Mute Climate for Change Special Edition

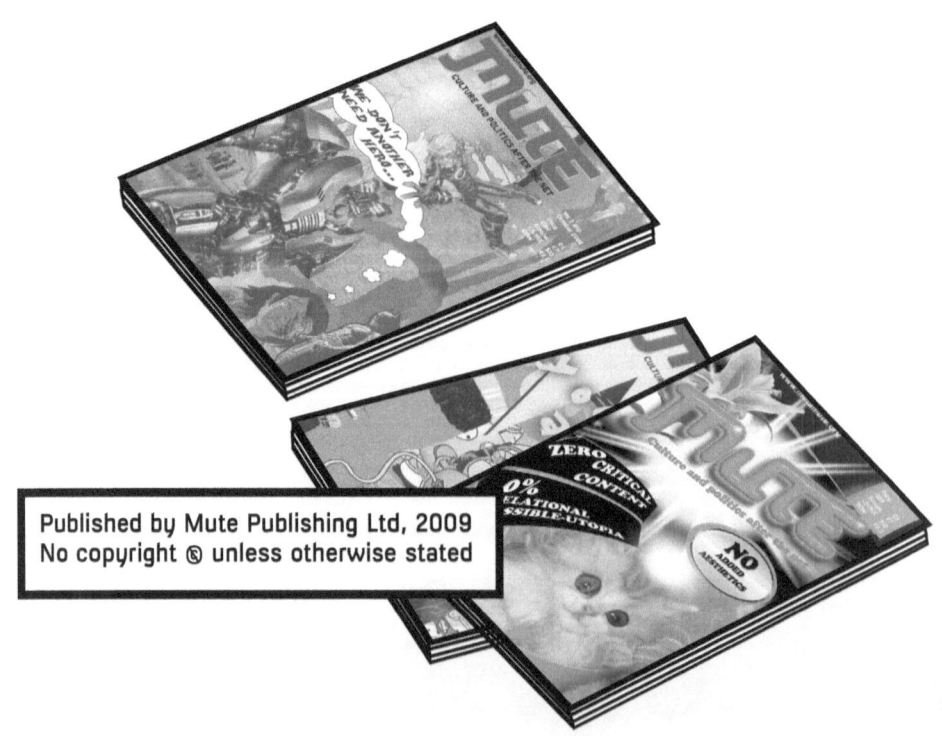

Published by Mute Publishing Ltd, 2009
No copyright ® unless otherwise stated

MUTE SPECIAL EDITION
CLIMATE FOR CHANGE

EDITOR
Josephine Berry Slater <josie@metamute.org>

EDITORIAL BOARD
Josephine Berry Slater, Matthew Hyland <infuriant@autistici.org>, Anthony Iles <anthony@metamute.org>, Demetra Kotouza <demetra@inventati.org>, Hari Kunzru <hari@metamute.org>, Melancholic Troglodytes <meltrogs1@hotmail.com>, Pauline van Mourik Broekman, Benedict Seymour <ben@metamute.org>, Stefan Szczelkun <szczels@ukonline.co.uk> and Simon Worthington

PUBLISHERS
Pauline van Mourik Broekman <pauline@metamute.org>
Simon Worthington <simon@metamute.org>

ISSUE DESIGN
Laura Oldenbourg <laura@metamute.org>, Simon Worthington and Alex Czincel <alexczin@web.de>

INTERNS
Olga Panadés & Paul Graham

OFFICE
Mute, Unit 9, The Whitechapel Centre,
85 Myrdle Street,
London E1 1HQ, UK
T: +44 (0)20 7377 6949
F: +44 (0)20 7377 9520
email: <mute@metamute.org>

SUBSCRIPTIONS
Howard Slater
T: +44 (0)20 7377 6949
F: +44 (0)20 7377 9520
email: <subs@metamute.org>
web: http://www.metamute.org/subs/

DISTRIBUTION UK
Central Books,
99 Wallis Road,
London, E4 5LN
T: +44 (0)20 8986 4854
F: +44 (0)20 8533 5821

CONTRIBUTING
Mute welcomes contributions of all kinds. Email <mute@metamute.org> with your ideas

You can also publish on Mute's website [http://www.metamute.org]. Post news, texts, events and comments, or upload media to the Mute Public Library http://pl.metamute.org

The views expressed in Mute and Metamute are not necessarily those of the publishers or service providers

Mute is published in the UK by Mute Publishing Ltd. and printed by OpenMute [http://openmute.org] print on demand (POD) book services in the USA and UK

COVER
Nils Norman. Thanks for playing along with our muppet madness!

ISBN 978-1-906496-29-6

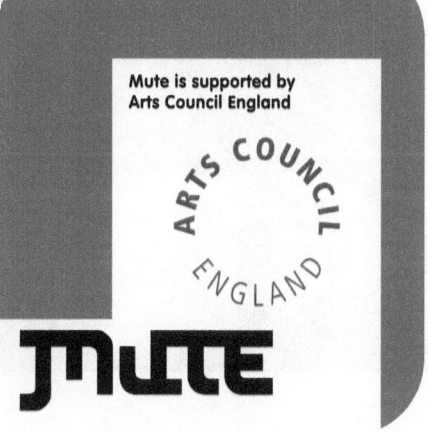

Mute is supported by
Arts Council England

Table of Contents

p.006 EDITORIAL
On the special issue Mute/FACT collaboration

p.042 PROMISED LANDS
Kate Rich on corporate IT's bad impersonation of neo-commoning

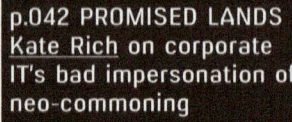

p.016 CAPITAL CLIMES
Will Barnes on the inhuman agent of global warming

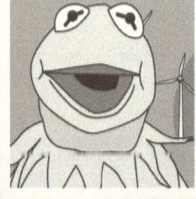

p.052 APOCALYPSE AND/OR BUSINESS AS USUAL?
George Caffentzis plots the Bush administration's green swerve

p.028 ACT MACRO
James Woudhuysen on technological alternatives to green austerity

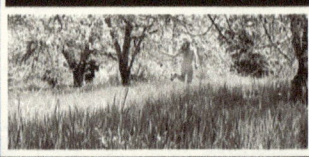

p.060 HEAVY OPERA
Anthony Iles reviews John Jordan and James Hewitt's climate change opera

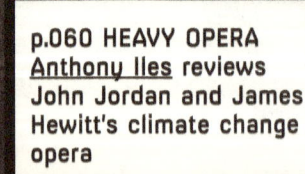

p.034
Tim Forsyth and Zoe Young on the mechanisms of global climate change governance

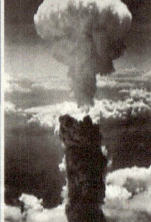

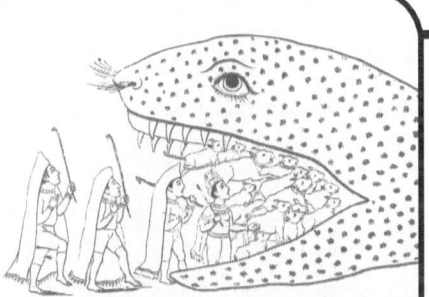

p. 070 SURVIVAL SCRAPBOOKS
Simon Yuill on Stefan Szczelkun's Survival Scrapbooks

p.108 CULTURE OF CAPITAL
Leo Singer & Claire Paillard on Liverpool City of Culture 2008

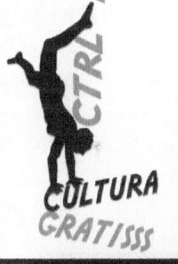

p.118 TAKE ME I'M YOURS
Anthony Davies exposes the neoliberal bottom line of 'progressive' cultural institutions

p.088 'OVERPOPULATION': LETTING CAPITALISM OF THE HOOK
Manchester No Borders on the controversial matter of so-called 'overpopulation'

p.096 A CLIMATIC DISORDER? CLASS, COAL AND CLIMATE CHANGE
John Cunningham on attempts to find a middle ground between trades unionists and environmentalists

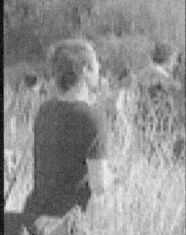

p.132 CLIMATE FOR CHANGE
Special FACT section

Editorial

EDITORIAL
by Josephine Berry Slater & Anthony Iles

Re-issuing *Mute*'s April 2007 issue on climate change now, in 2009, as a special edition in the context of FACT's Climate for Change exhibition is more than just an exemplary act of recycling. *Mute*'s online and print publishing activities can be understood as a kind of critical ecology in themselves, continually augmented by present conditions, projects and discourses. With its complete archive of published articles freely available online, *Mute* continually revisits and reassesses core themes and questions – climate change is one of those which perennially surfaces. Therefore this is no purely archival project, but one which allows the past to help the present by bringing articles published in the preceding two years into this new edition; moving the original issue on and making available the development of ideas and arguments that inform present day thinking.

By and large the writers in this issue of *Mute* accept that climate change is a reality. Earth's rising temperature can no longer be attributed solely to natural fluctuations produced by solar and volcanic activity, it is instead the result of man's massive consumption of fossil fuels. There are those who contest the science that underlies this idea, claiming that levels of CO_2 in the atmosphere follow rather than determine temperature – man's activity is irrelevant. Clearly this claim should be taken seriously, and not least because the outrage it provokes indicates the economic and political stakes of man-made climate change. Rather than the ultimate causes of global warming, however, our focus in this issue is the way its spectre is put to work by the developed world.

How this approach to climate change pans out will clearly be inflected by how much capitalism now, as opposed to two years before, is willing to spend time fixing the planet when at present it is busy fire-fighting within its own system. For the last

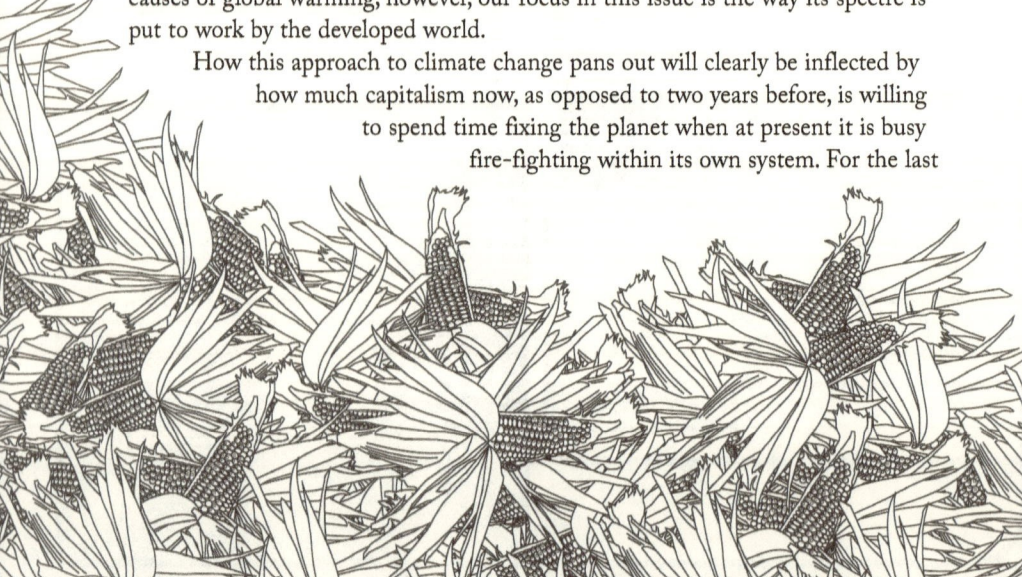

Josephine Berry Slater & Anthony Iles

two years news of an unravelling financial crisis has wiped climate change panic from the front page. However, the very way hysteria about environmental crisis preceded a liquidity crisis suggests that the steps corporations and governments were already taking towards a green agenda can be read very much in line with a crisis in the making. Enron, before it collapsed was, after all, one of the companies seen as an exemplar of green politics – by cutting production and speculating on reduced supply it was reducing energy output. Here the dangers of an intersection between the neoliberal project and green agendas are evident. Climate change gives the developed world licence to check and restructure development in the South, impose austerity measures on domestic populations, or to break its own dependency on oil-producing nations that won't, despite military intervention, tow the neoliberal line. Coupled with a global financial crisis, climate change now provides the alibi for capital to manage its crises in its own interests. Feeding Frenzy: Food, Fuel and Finance, a discussion hosted by *Mute* (July 2008), attempted to connect up these factors that govern our lives and think about how we could act to take control of them.[1] Rather than a total overhaul of the way we think about technology and how we produce, the current discourse only reiterates the broken economic system at the root of the problem and attempts to reform it.

This trend towards neoliberal reform and privatisation is increasingly visible in the way cities and cultural institutions are transformed. Leo Singer & Clara Paillard criticise the cultural ecology of a mega-event – Liverpool's Capital of Culture – in light of local anger over the management of regeneration projects and the city's housing provision. Anthony Davies examines the neoliberal turn in 'progressive' institutions – connecting up their hypocritical incorporation of politicised discourses in their cultural programmes with the unchecked deterioration of working conditions and privatisation within them. What is 'unsustainable' about the present organisation of the world is not only the pillage of the environment, but also the looting of communal resources and foreclosure of the possibilities for self-organised culture.

As George Caffentzis points out in these pages, the traumatic effects of climate change will not be felt by capital but by those it commands. It seems that this is already the case. While the fundamental imperatives of the global economic

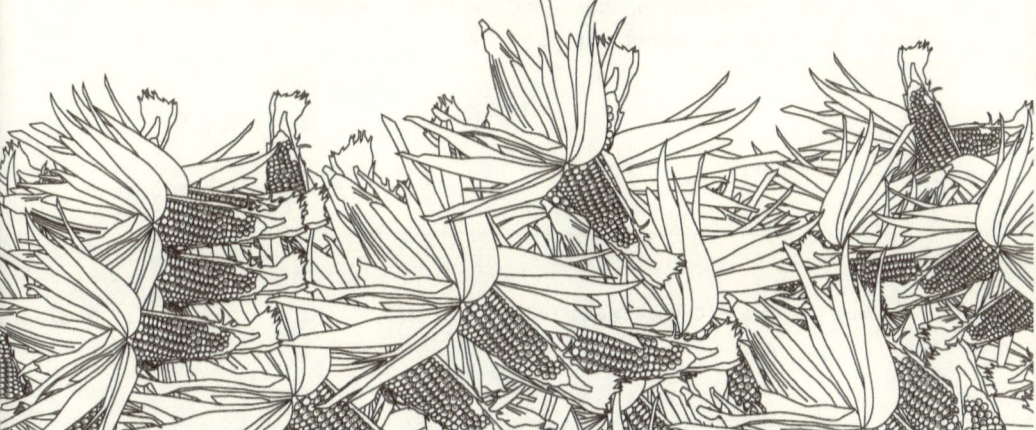

Editorial

system with its market (mis)managed allocation of energy resources remain unaltered, individuals in both the North and South are instructed to change their behaviour. While previously less powerful states were impelled to reorient their economies to dubiously 'greener' production, now major players are re-orienting themselves to a green-Keynesianism as the only solution to financial armageddon.

The world's poor will pay most dearly for what James Woudhuysen calls the 'micro-action' of governments, bearing the brunt both of what they do and do not do in response to the (ecological) crisis: the cost of maize, a basic food stuff, spirals as a result of the growth of the biofuel industry; green taxes and tariffs push up energy prices and the cost of movement; basic services such as refuse collection are cut. While recently energy prices have dropped dramatically in the face of falling demand as consumption contracts in response to the crisis, the possibility for an inflationary or even hyper-inflationary future remains. Meanwhile, nothing is done to address the threat of rising sea levels that will ravage coastal communities. As Zoe Young, Tim Forsyth, George Caffentzis and James Woudhuysen all argue, the new green order uses the threat of climate catastrophe to pursue other agendas.

A bleak picture to be sure. But there is hope in the recognition that global warming is not an inevitable consequence of human behaviour but rather the result of capital's inhuman drive to accumulate at any cost. In short, global warming is not made by man but by the capitalist mode of production. While insecurity of employment impairs the willingness and ability of labour to organise against capital, climate change is potentially a globally unifying lever for resistance. On the other hand, as capital pits whole regions against each other in the battle over development and control of energy resources, much of the left has pioneered (and recycles) the now dominant Malthusian moralism regarding behaviour modification and the need to limit consumption. Articles by Damian Abbott, on the Climate Camp 2007, and John Cunningham, on a meeting between mining and environmental activists this year, consider the challenges to protest movements of targeting 'global' issues, and show there is some potential for novel alliances in these unprecedented times. But, as Manchester No Borders point out with regard to the question of whether the planet is full, it is crucial to interrogate the premises and origins of received ideas within green and left discussions. If climate change is going to provide a focus for anti-capitalist struggle it must be seen for what it is – a problem of capitalism, not 'man' per se.

Footnote

1 http://linkme2.net/f5

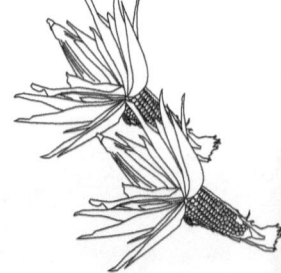

MEJAMUJE

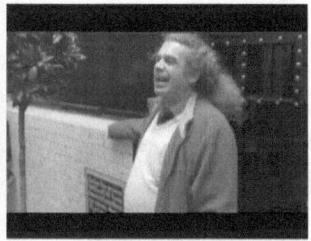

Video - Forever Blowing Bubbles: A Walking Tour with Peter Linebaugh and Fabian Tompsett (2008)
http://www.metamute.org/en/content/video_forever_bl owing_bubbles_a_walking_tour_with_peter_linebaugh_ and_fabian_tompsett_2008

A walking tour and talk in the City of London, taking in landmarks of capitalist crisis past and present. Writer Fabian Tompsett and Historian Peter Linebaugh gave a tour around the City relating the contemporary financial crisis to those of previous eras (such as the 1720 South Sea Bubble), using the urban fabric as text.

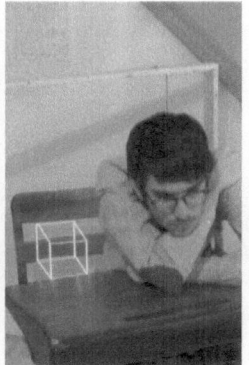

Code Dreams are Made of This
by M. Beatrice Fazi
http://www.metamute.org/en/content/code_dreams_are_ made_of_this

This year's Piksel festival celebrating 'Code Dreams' saw the boundaries between artists, audience, hardware and software blur in the collective pursuit of a machinic unconscious, as well as a highly conscious celebration of FLOSS culture.

Debt: The First Five Thousand Years
by David Graeber
http://www.metamute.org/en/content/ debt_the_first_five_thousand_years

Anthropologist David Graeber argues that it is only with a general historical understanding of debt and its relationship to violence that we can begin to appreciate our emerging epoch. Here he begins to fill in our historical knowledge gap.

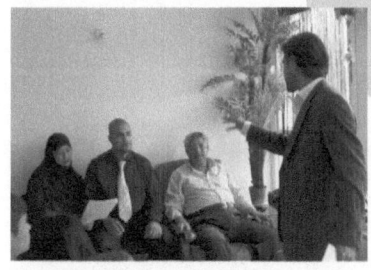

Brutalist Soap
by Kate Rich
http://www.metamute.org/en/content/brutalist_premolition

What lies beyond the failed utopias of the modernist welfare state and the free market? Gail Pickering's recent film/performance, despite its strictly internal focus on life inside a Brutalist housing estate, opens up scope for speculation.

http://metamute.org

palgrave
macmillan

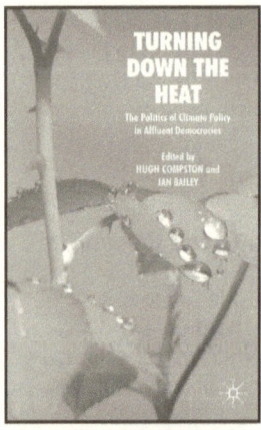
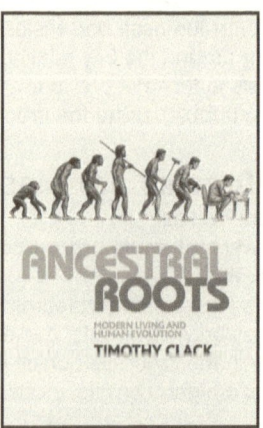
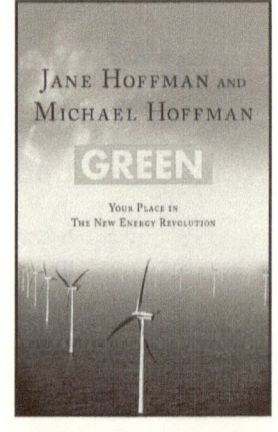
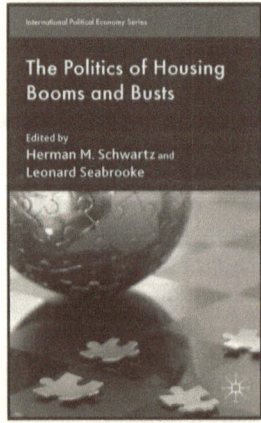
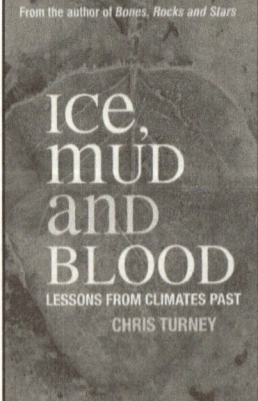
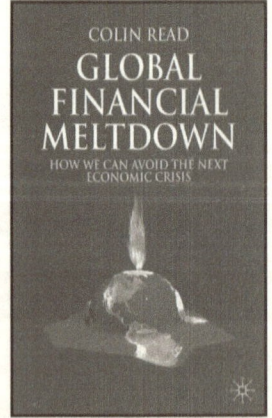

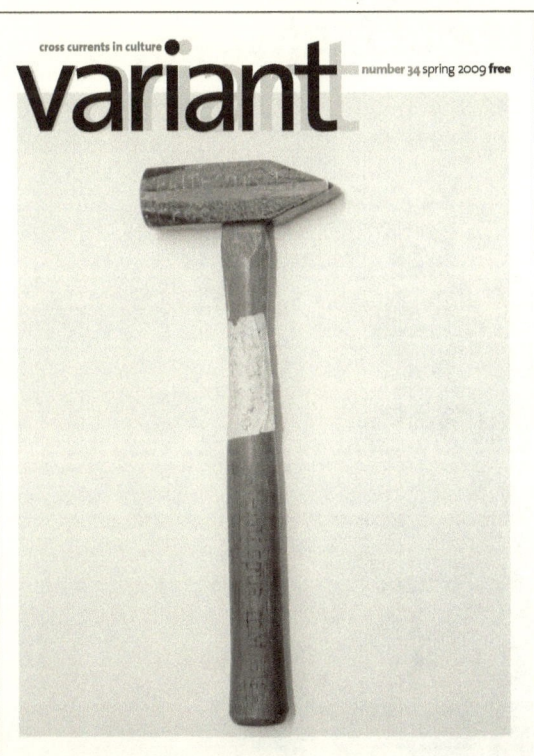

Culture in its broader social political context.

www.variant.org.uk

more is more

Independent media distribution & video screening network

More is More is an open source, online distribution system for small-scale and independent media. The aim of the network is to provide independent media producers and cultural organisations with a platform that can connect them to local outlets and events. More is More facilitates the sale of goods at such locations as well as direct through the website itself.

Commercial distributors are not best geared to the distribution of media products from the cultural, non-profit or political sectors. OpenMute's distribution network is an attempt to develop an alternative. More is More distributes the following: video, magazines, books, comics, posters, flyers and music. It is also possible to arrange your own event or film-screening through the platform.

While the site is at an alpha stage, we are looking for reactions and input from individual media-producers, cultural and activist organisations as well as a variety of outlets that might be interested in putting their products online or selling them locally.

An OpenMute project

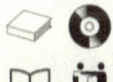

Supported by Digital Pioneers

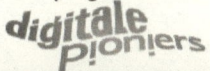

Fourteen years in a nutshell!
A new book about Mute...

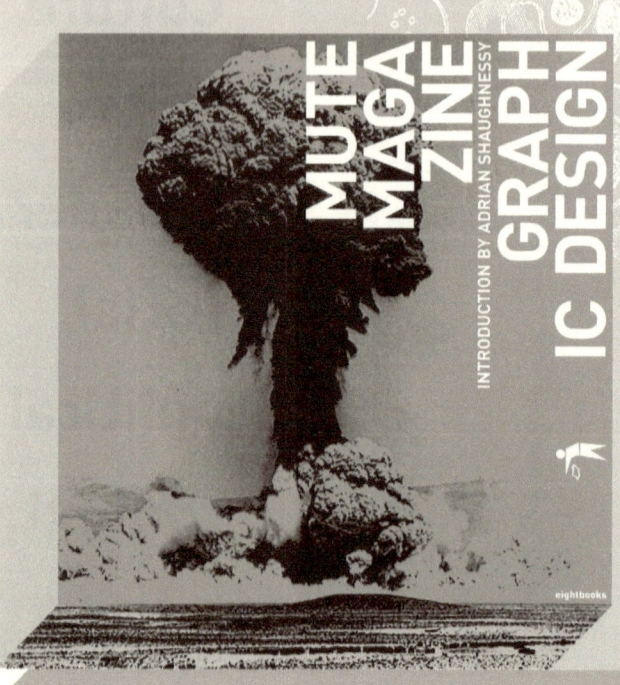

Mute Magazine: Graphic Design (April, 2008)

In the early 1990s, long before the internet became an integral part of life, a handful of pioneering magazines took it upon themselves to imagine the web into existence. Using fiction, interviews, speculative theory and experimental graphic design, London-based Mute wielded an influence disproportionate to its scale. Nearly fifteen years after its launch in November 1994, Mute's publication history defines an era, telling the fascinating tale of one publisher's relationship with the 'digital revolution'. This graphic design history presents a full overview of Mute's output, including logos, covers and spreads.

Introduction by Adrian Shaughnessy, with further contributions from Damian Jaques, Pauline van Mourik Broekman and Simon Worthington.

Published by 8books and now taking orders at Metamute.org/mutegraphics

Softback 220 x 220 mm, 144 pages, 250 colour Illustrations

10% discount for Mute subscribers

Buy it online at:
metamute.org/mutegraphics

UK £ 19.95	Europe €25
US $ 35	ROW €25

The long-awaited MUTE ANTHOLOGY out this May!

Proud to Be Flesh: A Mute Magazine Anthology of Culture and Politics After the Net
Eds. Pauline van Mourik Broekman & Josephine Berry Slater

Mute magazine was born, somewhere between art school anomie and the thrill of the World Wide Web's appearance, in 1994. Looking back, Mute's most unchanging feature is its wilful eclecticism and ceaseless criticality. Five years in the making, Proud to Be Flesh brings together the best articles to grace the pages of Mute in a single compendium. Featuring seminal writing on the evolution of Web 2.0, the knowledge commons, new media art, the politics of globalisation, and the material and immaterial ramifications of the net, Proud to Be Flesh is a one-stop reference to the cultural politics of the digital revolution. Thematically contextualised, this is an ideal resource for research, teaching, students, and readers craving a sustained and persistent analysis of 'culture and politics after the net'.

Chapter Titles:

1. Direct Democracy and its Demons: Web 1.0 to Web 2.0
2. Net Art to Conceptual Art and Back
3. I, Cyborg: Reinventing the Human
4. Of Commoners and Criminals
5. Organising Horizontally
6. Assuming the Position: Art and/Against Business
7. Under the Net – the City and the Camp
8. Reality Check: Class and Immaterial Labour
9. The Open Work

Available for pre-order in a hard cover, full-colour, ultra-limited edition.
Relive the best writing, graphics, and design of Mute
624 pages, 48 pages of illustrations
Pre-order price: £45.99 + p&p
Pre-order at: metamute.org/proud_to_be_flesh

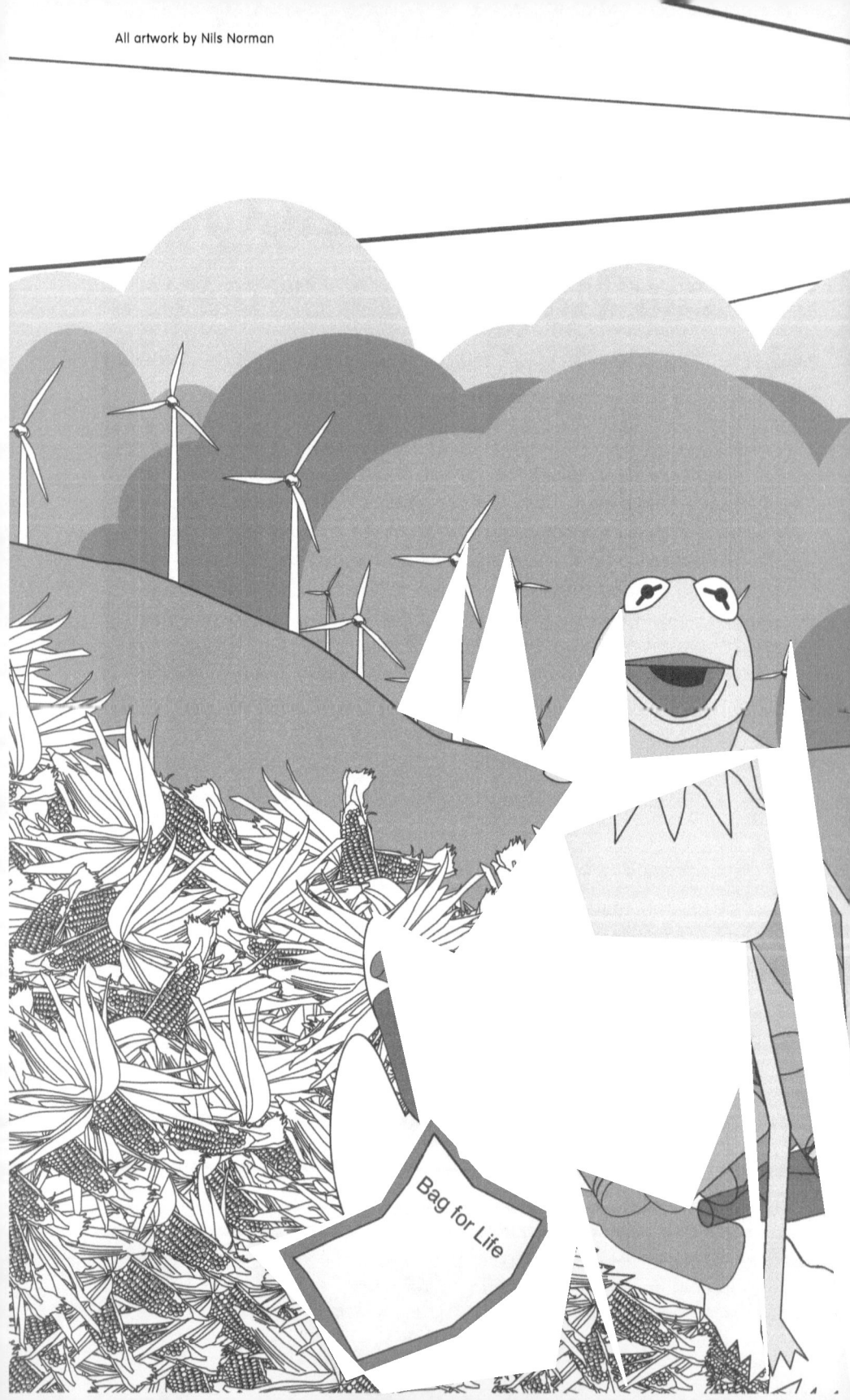

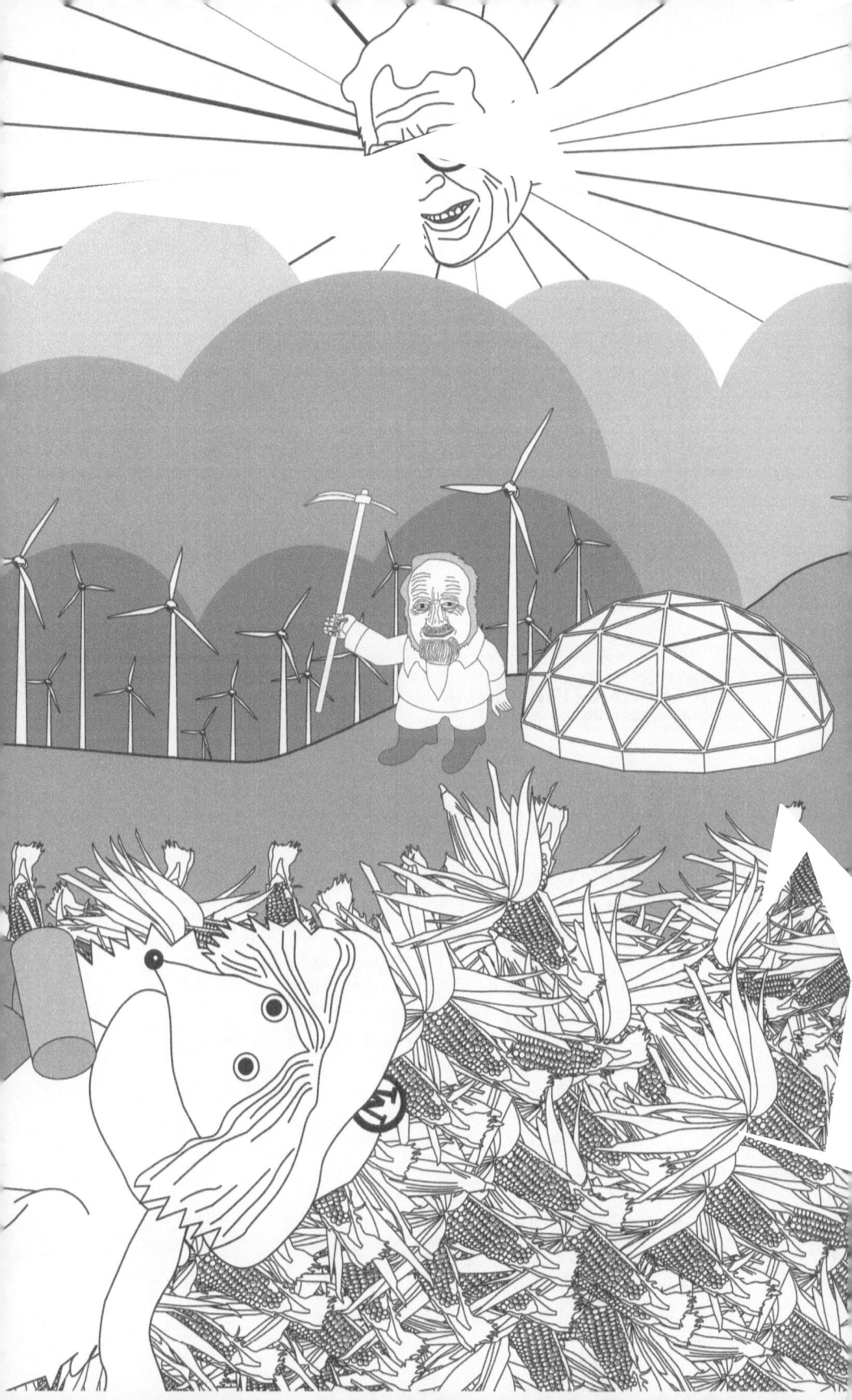

CAPITAL CLIMES

> Liberal critics assume that climate change is a 'man-made' process, not a natural phenomenon. Against this view, **Will Barnes** argues that global warming does indeed have an inhuman agent behind it – not nature but capital

Capitalist Criminality

With invaluable assistance from modern science and technology, capital is perpetrating a crime for which there is no name, the enormity of which has hitherto been and, apart from the literary holocausts of anti-utopian science fiction, largely remains unimagined.

Capitalist development, whether expanding or contracting and crisis-ridden, merely intensifies and exacerbates ecological degradation. The mindless and extraordinarily destructive disregard for the ecological consequences of the profitable pursuit of exploitable 'natural resources' has led, for example, to the consumption of hydrocarbon-based fossil fuels that are producing a warming of the earth that is melting the ice caps and raising sea levels, thus threatening the vast seaboard populations of the world. It has produced specifically the denuding of tropical forests, which, in the end, will deprive humanity of incalculable medicinal wealth. This pursuit has produced the strip mining and clear cutting of vast tracts of land – which have, in turn, created desertification rendering potentially agriculturally productive lands depleted. It has created a biotechnology centred on genetic engineering that has introduced transgenes transmitted through natural interspecies crosses which, in turn, have allowed emergence of resistant superweeds and superpests, which, in their turn, demand the application of further chemical poisons, i.e., herbicides and pesticides, that end up in groundwater, waterways and oceans and poison the food chain. The profitable pursuit of exploitable 'resources' of nature has further led to industrialisation of poultry and livestock production that, in the interests of a greatly enlarged worldwide markets for meat consumption (chicken, beef, pork), has generated life threatening strains of antibiotic resistant bacteria (E coli, Campylobacter, etc.) and highly pathogenic, potentially pandemic viruses. It has led to the massive and criminal termination of animal species and micro-biotic life forms, an extraordinary contraction in the very basis of life itself. More precisely, the pursuit of exploitable 'natural resources' for capitalist production on a world-scale has created a geological and biological regression reversing thousands and millions of years of natural evolution.

Indeed, species, new ones, comes into being and they disappear: Human beings, abrupt climatic changes, and even the occasional (by geological standards) natural calamity originating from beyond the earth in the solar system bring about extinctions, even the rare mass extinction. Yet, if the Arctic polar bear dies out (as a consequence of its inability to gain access to food sources as global warming melts the ice fields it uses to traverse distances and as a result of the early death of its young as PCBs, the product of industrial emissions that fall in their greatest concentration to earth in the Arctic, lodge in milk of lactating mother bears), it is an unnecessary loss of a majestic creature, one that is final. Extinct species do not make evolutionary reappearances. Nonetheless this loss, unintended and undesired, is not of the same order or magnitude as that at which bourgeois civilisation unknowingly takes aim. The problem is that specifically capitalist social transformations are borne along by an objective logic whose outcome is necessarily the very destruction of the natural world in its autonomy, cohesion, and otherness, that is, in its abiotic coherence, as living, and as a presupposition of specifically human life: It is the natural world as the totality of earthly nature (earthly nature as a totality and in its totality) that capitalist social transformation takes as its object.

The grand sweep of capital's movement at the beginning of the 21st century can only portend a future in which nature, because for capital nature is raw material for commodity production, at the very least undergoes continuous and ever greater homogenisation. Homogenisation means in the most minimalistic sense the ongoing destruction of ecological diversity, of species-specific ecological niches and, accordingly, species destruction. It entails, first, the loss of nature as an aesthetically beautiful setting and context in which human and other life forms live. Second, homogenisation of nature is characterised by the emergence and proliferation of a limited number of dominant species (e.g., coyotes, rats, starlings, cockroaches) that, highly adaptable to disrupted habitats, will be increasingly unsettling to life practices of other species. Third, it means the gradual disappearance of real, organic foundations of human (and generally animal) health and medicine as centres of biodiversity (such as the Amazon forests) disappear or collapse. Fourth, produced in and through the movement of capital, homogenisation of the earth will tend toward the creation of nature existing at two poles, uglified raw material basins (denuded forests, open mines, desertified grasslands, etc.) at the start of a cycle of commodity production and toxic wastelands and garbage cesspools (wetlands turned into landfills, decaying urban centres, vast stretches of ocean densely littered with plastic refuse, etc.) at the end of that cycle, i.e., with commodity consumption. Human beings acting and interacting in nature in this form will tend over several generations to become organically, physiologically, and perhaps even anatomically and morphologically a degenerating species.

The presupposition of homoeostatic, biospheric nature (i.e., nature as a self-regulating totality capable of internally modifying and adjusting its moments to maintain stability and equilibrium in the face of external changes, e.g., increases in ultraviolet radiation) is sufficient internal diversity. This diversity includes, among other things and relations, a variety of different climatic regimes and zones, a multitude of regional landscapes, and, centrally, a huge assortment of different life forms. Thus, it is precisely this internal diversity that the movement of capital is destroying and destroying independently of climate change, and, accordingly, it is the self-regulating character of nature, and life as it has developed over tens of thousands of millennia, that is disappearing.

Climate Change

What is important to recognise here is that the criminality of capital goes beyond the vast and potentially catastrophic problems that climate change has introduced. Even if societies of capital at the level of the world come to grips with ongoing climate change in a manner that allows them to maintain the 'achievements' of capitalism (densely populated reserve industrial armies and objective substance, i.e., built environment, means of production and the mass of circulating commodities) on capitalist terms, generalised ecological collapse as described above is encompassed by capitalist development itself, that is, by the practical reduction of surrounding nature to raw materials for capitalist production.

Let us, here and now though, consider climate change. The earth as we immediately apprehend it, what we call the biosphere, is a unitary phenomenon, its various partial systems (weather, oceans, atmosphere, abiogenic matter, organic life including 'man') are fully integrated and mutually dependent. It is a self-regulating 'system' whose internal diversity (precisely that which capital without regard to climate change is destroying) provides its own coherence and guarantees the preservation of life on earth. As the 'external envelope' of earth, it orders the constant energy inflow from space (solar energy) on which it is dependent. The constitution of earth's biosphere has qualitatively changed over geological time, meaning its composition, hence its structure (or the 'laws' governing its 'behaviour') has also changed. For any evolving, real totality such would have to be the case. What is basic for the earth as self-regularity is comprehended physically: The earth, from

> **Capital is the real subject of human society under conditions of capitalist production**

this perspective, is grasped as an energy system that makes 'self' adjustments to maintain an energy equilibrium (inflow of solar heat equals its outflow over time). Climate change is the mechanism of this adjustment, and climate is the immediate expression of this constitution of earth's biosphere.

To understand climate, and climate change, we must consider reconstructions of the earth's geography on a geological time scale. While the earth, at some 3.8 billion years of age, is estimated to be nearly as old as the solar system, geological dating begins in earnest 570 million years ago with the emergence of truly complex, highly developed life forms (fish, insects, reptiles). For the entirety of this vast sweep of geological time down to the present, we can designate 'cool' and 'warm' climate modes on earth. A simple determination of a climate mode is offered, namely, the presence of ice ... ranging from periods of intense glaciation (emanating from the poles covered with permanent ice caps) to phases in which the high altitudes have been seasonally cold. Tectonic activity, because it is capable of shifting continental-sized landmasses, has played the largest role in making possible intense cold, especially glaciation. For the latter only occurs when there are landmasses very near or over the poles. It should be obvious that over this simply enormous stretch of geological time, there were periods when landmasses were near or at the poles, and periods when they were not.

Antarctica split off from the ancient, gigantic continent known as Gondwana (encompassing present day Australia, Antarctica, South America, Africa and Asia Minor and Arabia) and arrived at it current locale over thirty million years ago. But by the time it reached what we identify as the southern pole it had already begun to glaciate (in response to tectonic changes, to plate uplifting and volcanism). The formation of the Southern Ocean, as an open waterway (with accompanying winds) sweeping round the earth, isolated Antarctica creating an atmospheric barrier against weather systems beyond this continent. Until recently, Antarctica has largely made its own climate, one very cold and dry, which, in turn, has helped cool an earth that hitherto (prior to its separation and drift) was warm and wet, Gondwana largely a temperate rainforest. Some twenty million years ago, tectonic activity entered a period, still ongoing, of considerable diminution (after the continents as we know them today formed), lessening, for the geological time being, its determination in the formation of climate. (Continental drift has brought large landmasses near to the poles thus allowing the earth's orbital eccentricity to cyclically create ice ages.) These cooler, drier conditions were particularly noticeable in Africa. And, under these newly forming climatic conditions, species, especially some of the truly large species (ancestors to many of today's large mammals who to them stand only as dwarf instances), died off and new ones appeared. Among the latter group were hominid lines, including the larger brained hominids who appear to be *our* ancestors.

Beginning about two and half million years ago, the dynamic climatic structure ('laws') characterising the most recent geological epoch stabilised. So what does our geologically 'contemporary' climatic structure look like?

For an answer to this question we must consider physical theory aimed at solving the problems of recurrent ice ages (glaciation). Today, our understanding of glaciation in the geological time frame we live in (it more or less slowly began fifteen million years ago) has largely been resolved into three great cycles that drive the earth's climatic variability. The earth's orbit around the sun is elliptical completing a cycle every 100,000 years. At its greatest as opposed to its smallest distance from the sun, a determination of the earth's eccentricity, there is a 20-30 percent reduction in the amount of radiation (heat) that reaches the earth. At that eccentricity, it is this relation (of sun to earth) that has produced ice ages at regular intervals over the past two thousand millennia. The second cycle concerns the tilt of the earth on its axis, its obliquity. Tilt determines where the most radiation from the sun will fall on the earth. A full cycle occurs every 42,000 years. As the earth revolves around the sun, tilt produces seasons. The last, shortest cycling, periods of 19,000 and 23,000 years, turns, so to speak, on the earth's wobble (called precession). Created by the magnetic mass distributed unevenly and off-centre between the earth's inner core and mesosphere, wobble creates a shift on average every 21,700 years in its 'true (celestial) north' (north determined along its axis in contradistinction from the Geographical North Pole) from Polaris to Vega. This shift affects seasonal intensity (e.g., hot summers, frigidly cold winters). In the case of all orbital cycles, the changes in radiation that reach the Earth are amplified by the amount present (more or less) of those gases, especially carbon dioxide, that trap solar radiation in the atmosphere.

We note that once the current warming synonymous with the last interglacial (the end of the last ice age ended roughly 11,600 years ago) was under way, 'archaic', stateless communities first began to form. Early

the self-regulating character of nature is disappearing

on during this interglacial (effectively extended by the greenhouse gas emissions warming of the last century and a half) the rudiments of agricultural, sedentary social life, the state and civilisation emerged for the first time.

Relative to over two million years of 'contemporary' geological time, historically constituted patterns of weather, such as the regularity of seasons each with its own predictable structure, are today disappearing. Instead, weather patterns that have existed over millennia are vanishing, and based on these vanishing patterns 'the weather' itself is losing its predictability. Similarly, climatic 'regimes' characteristic of specific geographical regions (e.g., a temperate region with mild summers and cold winters) are losing their defining features as these regimes become much more 'elastic'. Destabilised, under conditions of global warming induced climate change, the occurrence of weather at its extremes becomes more and more frequent (increased intensity of hurricanes in the Gulf and El Niño effects) because warming radically increases the moisture content in the atmosphere and thus produces extreme weather. (The unpredictability and extremism of global warming is perfectly consistent with instances of 'normality' by historical standards, e.g., frigid cold such as in Moscow last winter. It should be added that those extremes are not fixed. What is an extreme today may be 'normal' five years from now, and what is extreme then might very well hardly be conceivable today. In an abstract way, the only requirement for such warming is that over time the average annual temperature rapidly rises for the planet as a whole.)

Consequences – a 'New Nature'?

Climate change and in particular warming, as we now understand it, can be abrupt, occurring over years or

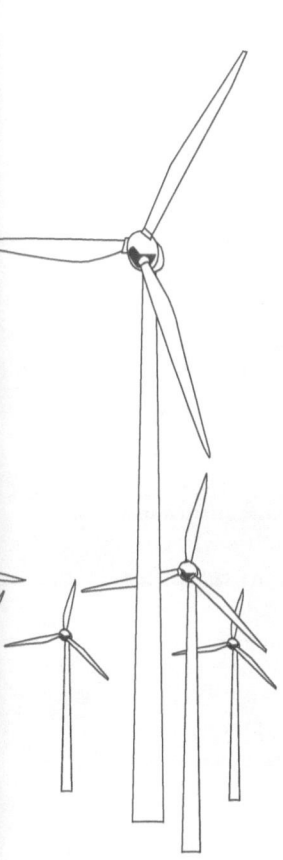

decades and not over millennia (or hundreds or maybe thousands of millennia). Abrupt climate change has certain 'tipping points' that 'force' change. Under geologically current conditions, there are three components of the self-regulatory system of the earth that are crucial for the constitution, if you will, of a 'new nature', that is, a different regime of climate, seasonality and weather. They are a shut down of thermohaline circulation in the North Atlantic (the Gulf Stream as it warms Europe, a shut down of which would be disastrous for Britain and North Europe), the destruction of the Amazon rain forests, and the release of gas hydrates (clathrates, ice crystal trapped methane, a carbon-based gas) from the ocean floors. All three are threatened by warming as it is generated by capitalist activity on the scale of the world. For example, sufficient warming (say, by no later than 2080) would melt enough of the Greenland ice sheet to shut down the Gulf Stream in the North Atlantic (melting of which pushes fresh water into the Stream's current – a vast conveyor of hot water from the Gulf, diluting the heavier because saline Gulf water, thus, preventing it from dropping toward the ocean floor in the area of Iceland, further preventing it from pulling more warm water in behind it, i.e., effectively shutting it down). The shut down would induce cooling which, in turn, would bring a halt to ice sheet melting that, in turn, would eventually restart the current and start a re-warming, all of which could go on for centuries until the ice reserve had reached a reduced threshold at which point it could no longer add enough fresh water to stop the circulation. Climatic see-sawing of this sort is one possible, under current conditions likely, outcome of warming. Climatic see-sawing is not, however, a lawful creation of a 'new nature', for example, a 'warm' or 'cold' mode, or better, as long as see-sawing continued, a new mode would not be firmly established, as climate at least in some parts of the world alternated between the two. (On the other hand, a massive release of clathrates premised on sufficient warming of the oceans, leading to species extinctions on the order of the Permo-Triassic extinction event, is another, this time abrupt, shift that could usher in a new climatic regime in just decades.)

Suspending consideration of the shape of a 'new nature', let us briefly reflect on the some of the features of warming as it is now occurring. These include, among others, increasing frequency and intensity of extreme weather (ice storms, hurricanes or cyclones, tornadoes spun from hurricanes, etc.), rising sea levels, and, possibly, the cooling of northern Europe (not to mention elsewhere the shift northward of subtropical seasonality and temperature into temperate zones).

To even the casual observer here in the United States, the incidence of extreme weather has qualitatively been on the upswing since the 1980s. For example, in 2005 the North-West experienced a severe winter drought; western states had a record heat wave in July; in the South-West, a marked increase in winter storms included record rain and snow; the central states had a major drought worsen throughout the summer; the South and South-East experienced a record number of hurricanes, fourteen, seven of which were major; and, the North-East had flooding in April and record precipitation in October... In two decades, rising sea levels will flood as much as a quarter of the land mass of Bangladesh; Dhaka, now on average 137 miles (221 kilometres) from the sea, will front the Bay of Bengal at 60 miles (97 kilometres); and, thirty million people will be displaced, countless others dead. Today, the freshwater wells immediately south of Dhaka have become increasingly saline, the water nearly undrinkable. Or, again, in two decades parts of Sydney, Australia, beginning from its harbour, will be underwater... As we write (28 February 2007), the temperature in London (latitude 51.52 °N) reached 47° F (8 °C); in the region of Moosonee (latitude 51.31 °N) in eastern Ontario at the southern tip of James Bay temperatures ranged from 9 to 14 °F (-13 to -10 °C). Both are roughly seasonal averages. And while London may generate 10F/6C degrees of its temperature as a consequence of its concentration of built environment, Moosonee is London's fate under conditions of a shut down of the thermohaline circulation in the North Atlantic.

'Man-Made' Climate Change?

The overwhelming consensus among scientists and spokespeople of capitalist states in the world today (and even in the U.S., Australia and Bangladesh among the most recalcitrant of states, there is grudging acceptance) that, in terms of causation, 'man' is responsible for warming induced climate change.

While the evidence is straightforward, the attribution both

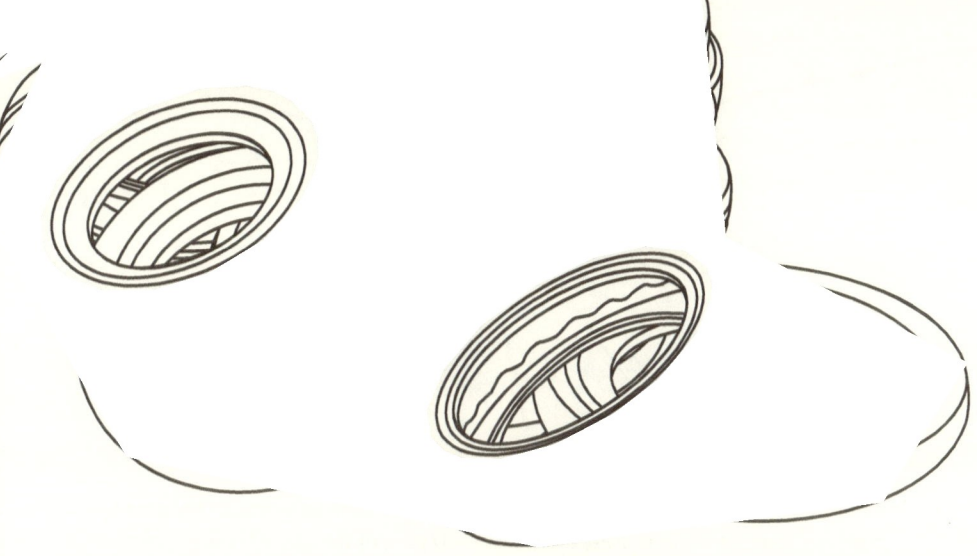

of culpability *and* the liable agent are effectively ideological, masking real agency and responsibility. Consider, first, the evidence.

From the outset of the current interglacial some 11,600 years ago down close to the end of the 18th century, average global surface temperatures have risen slowly, very slowly, but steadily. This increase, it should be noted, is relative. Plot the average from the peak of the last ice age (last glacial maximum) 22,000 years ago, and that incremental increase (circa 9600 BC to 1760 CE) is not noticeable. But plot average global surface temperature from 1760 to 1870 and the line of temperate approaches a positive 15° angle of incline. Plot it from there to the present and the angle of incline rises to roughly 45°. Back up and plot it from 8000 BC to the present, and those last 235 years present a nearly straight vertical rise.

Note the dates: As suggested earlier, circa 8000 BC is the point at which we mark the beginnings of sedentary agriculture, social division and the rise of the state. And 1760 marks that point at which we can date the commencement of the mechanisation of industry in the West (i.e., in capitalist England). In the former case, initial sedentary life and, with it, rising population began to generate a human input, methane (CH_4) and carbon dioxide (CO_2), into the atmosphere, nothing that before 1760 might delay a glaciation, but incrementally in the short view, noticeable. The development of capitalist industrial production after 1760, however, has indeed transformed the chemical make-up of the atmosphere. How?

On a geological time scale, atmospheric CO_2 has ranged from lows of 200 parts per million (ppm) during major glaciations to highs of 280-300 ppm during warm interglacials. Today, atmospheric CO_2 concentration stands at marginally more than 380 ppm, and is rising in geological terms at an extraordinary and

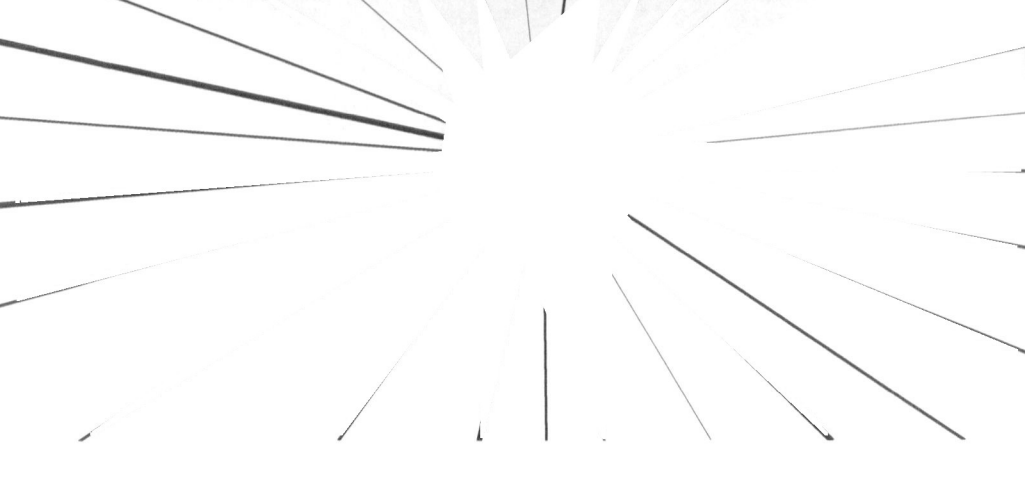

unprecedented rate with, at this moment, no end in sight. Best estimates put a tipping point (qualitatively hastening ice cap melting) as low as 480 ppm, reachable with even modern emissions reductions before 2080. This, then, is the major piece of evidence for anthropocentric based warming.

Second, consider the attribution of agency and, accordingly, responsibility for climate change. The Intergovernmental Panel on Climate Change tells us 'man', 'his' activity, is altering climate. In one sense, a very crude argument can and has been made (though not explicitly by the IPCC) that sheer human numbers, a global population of six billion, and the outputs that result from the volume of activity of so many people, bear direct responsibility. While the quality of human (animal and plant) life may well be grounds for limiting population growth, global warming does not result merely from the activity of masses of humans at any level of development: Today, an Indian child (the Indian subcontinent being one of the most densely populated regions on earth, India having the second largest population in the world) consumes 1/90th of the annual energy that her American counterpart does. The problem is forms of consumption, energy inefficient consumption not to mention profligate consumption, and the type of development that underpins that consumption.

If we have raised ourselves to the level of an understanding at which it is intuitively obvious that human population, either in the contemporary sense or the historical sense (going back some 10,000 years) or both, is neither the agent nor, accordingly, responsible for climate change, we have dissolved one mystification. 'Man' (here, human population generally) as such is a merely formal concept without a determinately real referent. Perhaps, then, the 'industrial system' is at issue. Or, perhaps, it is a question of 'man' in the 'industrial system'. In either case, we are dealing with empty abstractions. The issue is the historically specific configuration of groups of living men and women working within that 'industrial system', i.e., capitalist production. More precisely, the issue is the group which dominates that production. We refer, here, to those personifications of economic categories, capitalists (as well as the bloc of classes they have in tow). Capitalists (and states that unify otherwise disparate or competing capitals) make decisions concerning the allocation of monies and capital, concerning what and the manner in which 'natural resources' are exploited and utilised, and concerning the technologies on the basis of which those activities are carried out. Still, it is not just those decisions, but the entire system of social relations, that is at issue in climate change. In this sense, it is the subject of society (a part of nature, yet confronting it as raw material for the production of commodities) that is the agent responsible for climate change. It is not 'man' that is remaking, as it were, the biosphere; that remaking is a product of 'his' own objectified and alienated power. This power is capital: Capital is the real subject of human society under conditions of capitalist production (real domination).

At the 'price' of cataclysmic human and social costs abrupt climate change could transform the geography and sociology of social life: Over the period of decades, a qualitative increase in regimentation and repression of domestic populations to insure compliance with draconian restrictions on energy consumption; drought and starvation, massive, unnecessary death; depopulation of coastal areas around the world, forced dislocation, creation of huge frontier zones and camps of displaced persons along national borders, refugees in the tens of millions living in squalor without hope, resource wars between states, ethnic cleansing and genocides as a regular feature of daily life. Nonetheless, while capital *cannot* stem the ecological collapse which its very movement is engendering and within which climate change is situated, it can and, in our view, will meet the warming-induced, climate crisis. Whatever else, the social relations of capitalist production will neither disintegrate nor disappear in the maelstrom of climate change.[1] The real question is whether capital, at unimaginable human cost, will set the terms on which this change is confronted, or whether we shall.

Footnote

[1]
In the imperialist centre of global capitalism, governed by that most backward, obstinate of regimes, capital has begun to weigh in. As we write, TXU Corp., a Texas-based energy conglomerate is being sold to a group of finance capital-based private investors in the largest ever private equity deal. The new investment group promises not to build eight out of eleven proposed coal-fired power plants, and to double its investments in wind power and the creation of internal efficiencies qualitatively reducing emissions; at the same time, independently of the American State at the national level, five western state governments including California have signed an agreement to reduce greenhouse gas emissions.

Will Barnes <wwbarnes@yahoo.com> is a long-time activist living in the northern United States

> The emerging capitalist War On Global Warming concentrates on adapting technology and behaviour – particularly other nation-states' – to mitigate environmental damage. Transformative technological and social innovation is better than meddling micro-action, argues James Woudhuysen

ACT MACRO: TECHNOLOGICAL ALTERNATIVES TO GREEN AUSTERITY

A ngela Merkel is chancellor of Germany, a Christian Democrat and a physicist. She also believes in 'outreach'. Germany's outreach programme with China, India, Mexico, Brazil and South Africa, she says, allows it to sound out these nations about their 'general readiness to act' about climate change. Merkel warns Beijing not to put economic growth ahead of climate change, she warns Russia to let EU energy firms get firmer roots on to its soil. She insists that globally tradable emissions trading certificates are the 'most sensible instrument' to cut CO_2 and 'a very-market friendly one'. She wants a December 2007 UN conference in Bali to begin the 1-2 year process of drawing up a treaty on climate change to succeed the December 1997 Protocol to the United Nations Framework Convention on

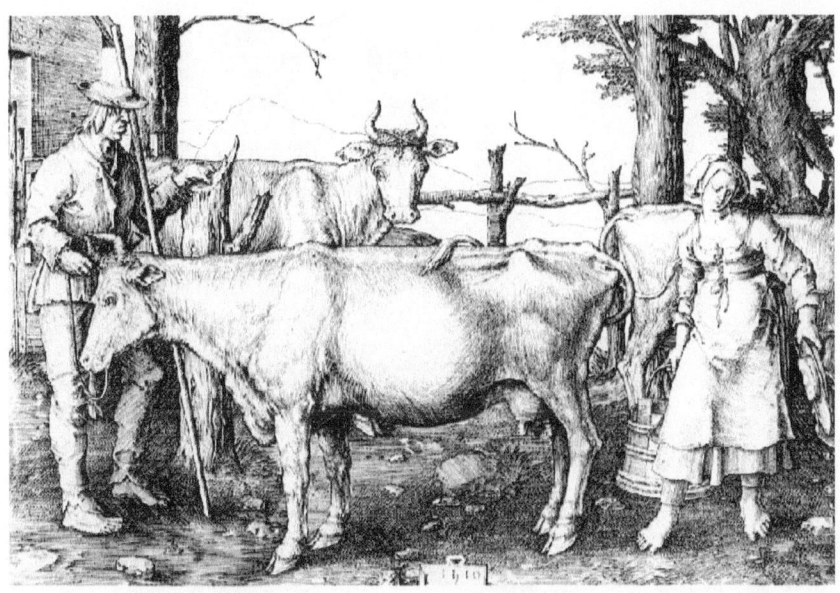

Climate Change – the Kyoto Protocol, which will expire in 2012. Invoking the Stern report on the economic impact of climate change as her 'main paradigm', she argues that 'whatever happens', the cost of 'inaction' on climate change will be higher than just muddling through.[1]

It is nice to know that nation states' invention of a market for a particular kind of molecule is a market-friendly move and a fine example of the 'action' that is now required on climate change. It is also nice to hear Germany and the EU lecture the developing world about how they should develop. But in fact lectures come very easily to Greenish governments. Even environment minister David Milliband, relatively an extremist among ministerial carbonistas, has felt called upon to warn Greens – and perhaps himself – not to be 'bossy'.

In fact all-round economic development and all-round technological innovation are the only actions that can deal properly with mankind's problems – of which global warming is one among many. The actions that Merkel proposes are about clipping coupons and austerity, especially in what used to be called the Soviet bloc and the Third World. If Germany gets its way, coal-dependent Poland and China will both suffer. Indeed, Clean Green Angela wants Europe to export, to these countries, the Clean Green technologies in which Germany specialises, and which it believes will be Good For Them.[2]

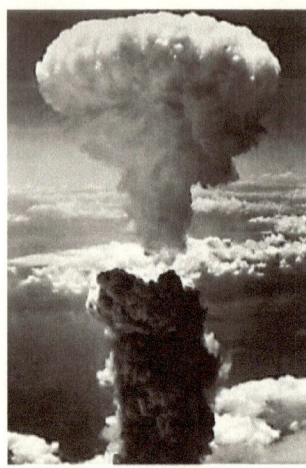 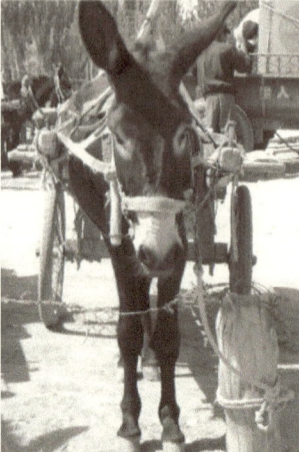 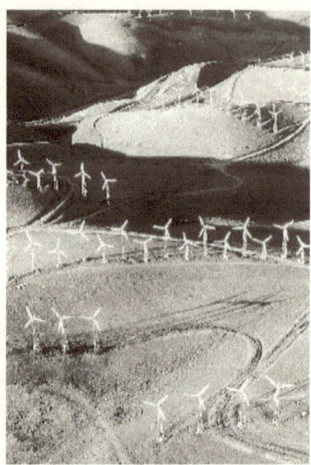

To raise the share of renewable resources in Europe's energy mix to 20 percent by 2020 is now the EU's highest goal. Yet the innovations with which the Brussels Commission proposes to meet that goal are not very ambitious. Its Energy Policy for Europe mentions wave and tidal power just once: the costs of photovoltaic, solar thermal power, and wave and tide power are, it opines sagely, 'projected to decrease from currently high levels'. It believes that all new coal-fired plants in the EU should to be fitted with CO_2 capture and storage, and that 'existing plants should then progressively follow the same approach'. When by? Oh, maybe by 2020 again.[3]

There is some money going into Green innovations. Not just the Toyota's hybrid Pious car, but also cars made by Ford and other major manufacturers, are becoming ever more energy-efficient. But generally Merkel's oh-so-activist, insurance-policy approach to climate change can only make commitments to high-tech environmentalism falter. If Battersea is ever revived with all-green technology, Greens would still object to the scale and urban location of the endeavour. We should, equally, never imagine that restrictions on car and airline use – road pricing, taxes on those stag-night flights to Tallinn – will lead to more investment and technology in public transport, and in particular, on the railways. After all, Mike Mitchell, the director-general of the Department for Transport's rail group, has told the House of Commons public accounts committee that peak-time rail commuters should expect to stand on their journeys for up to 30 minutes at a go.[4]

The evidence is that corporations and governments are only belatedly, and in a very narrow and leisurely manner, investing in relatively small projects to advance Green technologies; technologies that are more about raising awareness and controlling consumer behaviour than they are about fulfilling the world's need for more energy and less carbon. But there is a wider perspective that is needed here. If modest, behaviourist technological development – metering your every use of energy every minute of the day, for example – eludes the capitalists, how much more tentative will they be about the comprehensive programme of technological innovations needed to raise Africa from famine and Indonesia from disasters? Solve those truly colossal

we need a 'can do' attitude to nuclear power and nuclear waste

problems in a spirit of adventure rather than insurance, and global warming will be solved in the process.

What are the main outlines of such a programme? What we need is progress across both the energy sector and beyond.

In energy, we need to give up on micro-generation – the subject of a princely £50m from Gordon Brown in his March 2006 Budget – and instead move toward macro-generation. That means large-scale wave, tidal and off-shore wind. It means large-scale cultivation of biofuels, and perhaps genetically modified biofuels, too (though we all know someone who has died because of these). It means city-wide schemes for Combined Heat and Power. In the longer term, we need to make fewer sneers about the possibility of nuclear fusion: an international budget 10 times the Iter organisation's £7bn for demonstration fusion in the south of France shouldn't be too much to ask. And right now, we need a 'can do' attitude to nuclear power and nuclear waste.

Wind, solar, wave and tidal energy are intermittent sources of power, and need clever geographical dispersal, mutual complementarity and large-scale back-up power sources if they are to provide energy on any kind of reliable basis. As the science writer Joe Kaplinsky points out, it is true that other scale technologies generate more energy – Drax, the largest coal power station in the UK, makes four Gigawatts of electricity, and the Itaipu dam in Brazil and Paraguay boasts 11 Gigawatts. But at 1 GW, a typical nuclear power station easily beats the 310MW of electricity made by the largest solar installation in the world (over seven sites in the Mojave desert, California), and also exceeds the 735MW racked up by the largest wind farm in the world (Horse Hollow Wind Energy Center, Texas).

Nuclear power isn't a silver bullet. No doubt it will take its place among other energy technologies, old and new. But in terms of output and in terms of familiarity, it has a lot going for it. The next ('Generation IV') nuclear systems may, too, finally prove fully economic to run.

Turning now to nuclear waste: The

UK has a historic legacy of high and intermediate level nuclear waste that, in volume terms, is estimated to total 475,000 cubic metres of the stuff.[5] But how much is 475,000m3? Take the cube root of that, and it's 78 metres. In other words, all the existing bad and really bad nuclear waste in the UK, generated over more than 50 years, occupies a volume well under 100x100x100 metres.

And the new waste that an ambitious nuclear programme would generate is pretty modest too. Modern nuclear plants produce significantly less waste than earlier types. The UK's official Committee on Radioactive Waste Management suggests that if the current level of nuclear capacity were replaced with new-build, existing waste stocks would increase by about 10 percent by volume. The UK would have to add a 36x36x36 metre cube of nuclear waste – divided up, to be sure – on top of its existing 78x78x78 one.

To store this very modest amount of nuclear waste should not be beyond even British engineers. Are we saying that, in the 21st century, handling these amounts of waste is beyond the wit of man? And there are other possibilities. At Ruhr University in Bochum, Germany, Professor Claus Rolfs has begun experiments in cooling the products of fission in metal, so as to encourage them to accelerate their rates of radioactive decay, and so lower radioactive half-lives.[6]

Everywhere in energy innovation there is minimal impact and maximum regulation

Beyond energy, we need to tackle the root causes of backwardness around the world, and not get hung up on how climate change supposedly makes them worse. Was it really climate change that led to massacres in Darfur, or the plight of the Palestinians? Or are there more fundamental injustices at stake here, which an obsession with carbon will do little to relieve?

In agriculture the starving countries need mechanisation, not what junk-mail inserts in British magazines tell us they need – ploughs, donkeys, hand-drawn wells. In hydrology we need to save more than Venice, and do it with more than a charitable donation at Pizza Express.

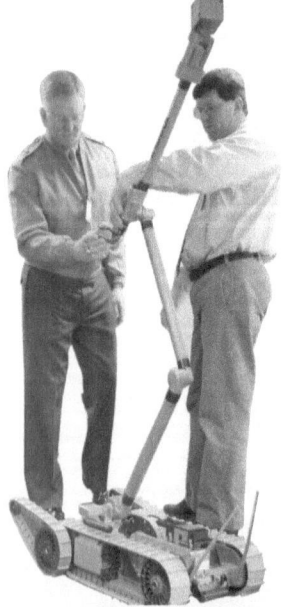

Image: iRobot's floor care robot

Among older people we need to build on the way the US firm iRobot has sold more than two million floorcare robots. We need to think about how today's manufacturing techniques, which allow Boeing to make planes on a moving assembly line, can also help meet the UN's estimate of the 100,000 new homes the world needs to build every day to meet popular demand.

By thinking big and having faith in our talents, a programme of transforming the planet in the direction of humanism could do much for energy supply and carbon reduction. But can US, Chinese or Indian capitalism really deal with this kind of challenge?

The evidence is that they cannot. In fact, as we have seen, they have taken a cautious, gingerly attitude even to Green technologies, let alone transformational ones.

Since the end of the Cold War and 9-11, the capitalists have lost their nerve. But that's their problem, not ours. Mao Tse Tung's dumbed down slogan, 'Serve the people' has been transformed into 'Slave for the planet' – walk everywhere, consume less, don't overpopulate the land, reduce your footprint, bend over and grow your own food. Everywhere in energy innovation there is minimal impact and maximum regulation.

These are dark days. Happily, though, it will be up to us, not governments and imperialist NGOs, to do the big stuff that tomorrow's youthful billions will demand.

Footnotes

1
'German chancellor lays our roadmap to follow-up treaty on climate change', *Financial Times*, 7 March 2007.

2
'Merkel to press for EU deal on climate', *Financial Times*, 7 March 2007.

3
Brussels Commission, 'An Energy Policy for Europe', 10 January 2007, on http://ec.europa.eu/energy/energy_policy/doc/01_energy_policy_for_europe_en.pdf

4
Robert Wright, 'Row as commuters told: don't expect a train seat', *Financial Times*, 18 January 2007.

5
DTI, 'Energy Review: the Energy Challenge', 11 July 2006, p.118, on http://www.dti.gov.uk/energy/review/index.html

6
Institute of Physics, 'Cool Solution to Waste Disposal', Press release PR22(06), 1 August 2006, on http://www.iop.org/Media/Press%20Releases/press_6762.html . Professor Rolfs: 'We are currently investigating radium-226, a hazardous component of spent nuclear fuel with a half-life of 1600 years. I calculate that using this technique could reduce the half-life to 100 years. At best, I have calculated that it could be reduced to as little as two years. This would avoid the need to bury nuclear waste in deep repositories — a hugely expensive and difficult process.'

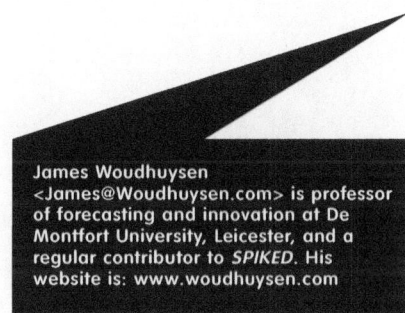

James Woudhuysen <James@Woudhuysen.com> is professor of forecasting and innovation at De Montfort University, Leicester, and a regular contributor to *SPIKED*. His website is: www.woudhuysen.com

CLIMATE CHANGE CO₂LONIALISM

In their tango with grassroots green activists, inter-governmental policy makers are taking the lead. Tim Forsyth and Zoe Young analyse the 'new green order' and the carbon offset colonialism that accompanies it

Tim Forsyth and Zoe Young

According to Tony Blair, the climate change debate is 'finally over.' Who can dismiss the economic arguments of the *Stern Report on Climate Change*? Only a Channel 4 controversialist or two, perhaps, and a few (mainly oil-funded) scientists. The bigger policy debate, about who should carry the burden of tackling the problem, should now begin. Instead, however, there seems to be consensus among global elites about where to start (be afraid, be very afraid ... but always trust the government), how to address the challenge (change development patterns in the South to 'offset' carbon emissions produced by business as usual in the North), and who is responsible (mainly you and me). Real doubts and arguments are suppressed while market-friendly 'solutions' are served up on a nice, glossy plate. Last time western Greens had the ear of their governments it lead to the creation of the World Bank's Global Environment Facility (GEF). Today, this 'new green order' is still evolving before our fearful, blinkered eyes.

This 'order' limits space for collective rethinking of energy, production or consumption policies. There is no room to challenge the political assumptions that inform them nor the pattern of investment in public energy infrastructure. Mainstream 'climate' discourse focuses instead on marginal interventions such as switching to more efficient light bulbs and expanding pine plantations. For as long as the 'logic' of capitalist economic expansion remains unchallenged, it seems hardly possible for high energy-consuming societies to adapt in time to escape a grim Malthusian fate. But Malthus wanted to be proved wrong, and if brave, we still could be.

a 'new green order' is evolving before our fearful, blinkered eyes

According to the first assessment in 1990 by the Intergovernmental Panel on Climate Change (IPCC), the scientific body responsible for assessing recent research into climate change, Green House Gas (GHG) emissions had to be reduced by 60 percent below then current levels in order to prevent dangerous climate change. In 1999, Greenpeace said that only about 25 percent of declared fossil fuel reserves can safely be burnt; the New Economics Foundation noted in 2006 that the demand reduction required in the oil sector is now five or six times that resulting from the OPEC oil price hike of the 1970s. Even the Stern Report, with its 'old economy' rationale, noted this year that

> the stocks of hydrocarbons that are profitable to extract [under current policies] are more than enough to take the world to levels of greenhouse gas concentrations well beyond 750 parts per million of carbon dioxide [a 'safe' level has been set as 450ppm].

If governments were to follow the advice of these experts they might work less from the premise of what big business wants today than from a calculation of how much oil, coal and gas *can* still safely be burnt, and then allocate the remaining energy across our species' basic needs: food, shelter, warmth, fresh water, health care, sanitation, security and a minimum of entertainment and travel for all.

> 'Our countries are not toilets for your emissions!'

Instead, the Kyoto Protocol is the main international agreement to address the threat of anthropogenic climate change. If you read the BBC News website or *The Independent* newspaper, you would think that supporting Kyoto is an acid test of green credentials. But what would Kyoto achieve, were it fully implemented? Signed in 1997, it came into force in 2005, and committed the world's industrialised countries to reducing

Tim Forsyth and Zoe Young

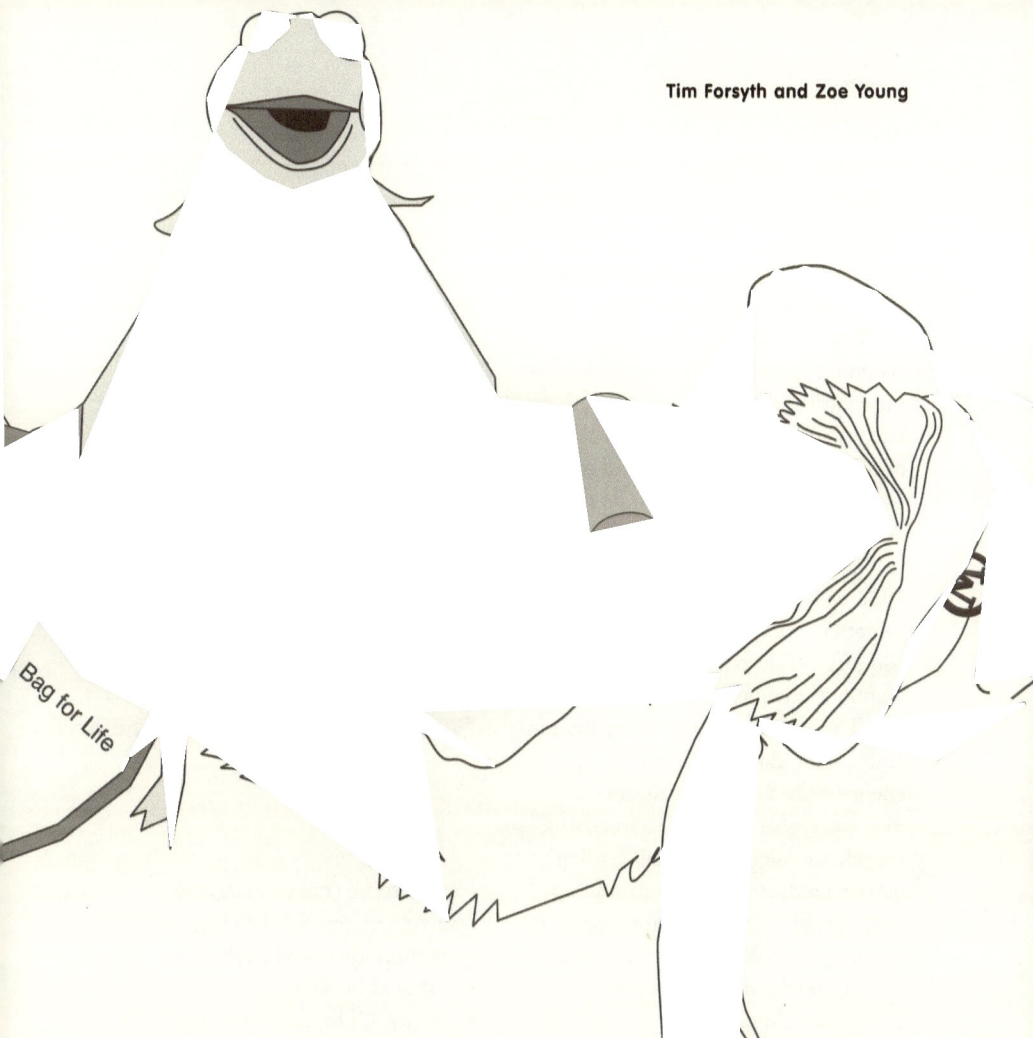

greenhouse gas emissions just 5.2 percent by 2012. Now the USA and Australia have pulled out, and only a few European countries are likely to achieve their target.

Debate about how to achieve even these minimal reductions is barely off the starting blocks. We now know it is up to us to use alternative light bulbs, green energy companies etc., or even to offset our emissions on the carbon market.

Meanwhile, tax and subsidy incentives for big companies to shunt ever more goods around the world in pursuit of comparative commercial advantage remain in place, and publicly funded international financial institutions such as the World Bank still invest billions of dollars in oil and gas development – many times more than they devote to energy efficiency measures or renewable energy technologies.

Radicals have no effective space other than the streets in which to challenge the elite's preference for economic growth at all costs. Interim mechanisms designed to 'do something' and yet still maintain the political status quo are constantly renewed and re-advertised. Each is shown to be as empty as the last (for example, the GEF, inaugurated at the Rio Earth Summit in 1992, is underfunded and now almost forgotten – despite its claims to the contrary) while ever more glossy 'solutions' emerge.

The latest of these is the market in emissions 'indulgences' for the energetically sinful. The 'flexible mechanisms' of the Kyoto Protocol include so called 'Emissions Trading' between industrialised countries that have agreed to set targets for reduction. In this system, Russia and the Ukraine were allowed 0 percent growth on their 1990 levels. At present, these countries now emit about 25 percent less CO_2 than in 1990 because of deindustrialisation following the collapse of the Soviet Union. Under 'Emissions Trading', Russia and Ukraine can 'sell' this 25 percent reduction to governments who continue to pollute, as if it reflected genuine energy saving and reduced emissions. Critics call this the 'hot air' problem, the exchange of certificates for reductions that would have happened anyway. Overall energy use – and hence GHG emission – is not reduced thanks to this highly flexible mechanism.

Other 'climate-friendly' investments are available under schemes called Joint Implementation (JI) and the Clean Development Mechanism (CDM). These allow industrialised countries to

carbon forestry is CO_2lonialism

achieve some emission targets by investing in renewable energy or plantation forestry abroad. (JI is investment between industrialised countries; CDM involves investment from North to South).

The idea is that policy should encourage emission-reducing investments wherever they are cheapest. This logic is valid on some levels, but can be criticised for picking the 'low hanging fruit'. Unfortunately, many such projects are also not properly monitored, and who knows what happens to the 'benefits' once the initial, publicly advertised phase is over. Fixing carbon into soil and forest plantations is not straightforward and requires fast-growing trees with little disturbance;

usually monocultures, requiring high water, fertiliser and pesticide inputs to survive, with all the social and environmental consequences implied.

Some critics suggest that offset forestry's ability to absorb carbon can be exaggerated because protecting, or planting, forests in one region may displace deforestation to other regions. It is also not always clear that the companies involved have full rights to the land – in Brazil for example, ownership of much of the land used for plantations is contested since the time of the dictatorships, if not the original conquistadors. Executed cheaply by companies who make a business out of pulp or charcoal, such plantations tie up land into a forest monoculture that would otherwise be wild nature with all its joys and benefits, or used for vital agricultural development.

These topics have provoked intense emotions, and popular resistance. One climate change negotiator from an African country angrily told participants at a London meeting, 'Our countries are not toilets for your emissions!'. Farmers, ecologists and trade unionists in South America have formed the 'Alert Against the Green Desert' network and take action to counter conversion of large areas of land to plantations.

Some political intentions underlying carbon-offset forestry are fairly clear. The environmental writer, Larry Lohmann, reported a US Department of Energy official as saying 'tree planting will allow US energy policy to go on with business as usual out to 2015.' Rightly or wrongly, these statements create fear that more industrialised countries are not interested in addressing climate change, or in encouraging 'development-friendly' investment in the South. Various critics say carbon forestry is 'CO_2lonialism'. Some southern governments, notably Costa Rica, have welcomed forestry-based projects; their potential for creating rural livelihoods, or playing a part in a climate policy portfolio, should not be dismissed. But forestry in itself is not going to bring about real change.

At the end of Al Gore's film *An Inconvenient Truth* he lists ten simple action points. These include using less hot water, recycling more, driving less, and planting a tree, with the advice that 'a single tree will absorb a ton of CO_2 over its lifetime.' But some wise elders in Britain may remember the phrase, 'Plant a tree in '73' – and if it didn't stop climate change back then, why should it do so now?

Lester Brown of the Worldwatch institute said in 2005:

> If [China] consumes paper at the same rate we [in the US] do, it will consume twice as much paper as the world is now producing. There go the world's forests. If the Chinese then have three cars for every four people – as the US does today – they

would have a fleet of 1.1 billion cars, compared to the current world fleet of 800 million.

Clearly, policies adopted in China will be crucial. But portraying this country as the problem seems to give credibility to the belief that industrialisation is a club only for the richer world.

Western governments' climate change policy should probably stop evaluating success in terms of reducing the level of GHG in the atmosphere. Seeking to reduce hypothetical concentrations without understanding the local impacts of these projects will simply undermine the political accord necessary to move forward together.

The same problem occurs with the Stern Report which, like many economic projections, uses a 'discount rate' to calculate the cost of future damage from climate change today. This assumes a conformity in the effect of climate change on different populations, and overlooks the way that palliative projects may create problems of their own. Powerful figures such as Nicholas Stern might be advised to stop treating climate change as a universal risk, addressed by general reductions in energy use or emissions generation, and instead seek more equitable solutions that reduce real people's risk of living a degraded existence.

The Executive Board of the CDM has often argued that investments in industrial technology are preferable to simply sequestering CO_2. For example, many companies have sought financial support under the CDM for flaring methane gas from landfills (methane has a global warming potential 23 times the value of CO_2, and so flaring may mitigate climate change by effectively converting methane to CO_2). But critics suggest that flaring misses the opportunity to use this gas for local heat or electricity generation. Under the Kyoto Protocol, there are no obvious incentives for such moves. Rather, all CDM projects have to pay 2 percent of profits towards an 'Adaptation Fund', money for long-term developments such as reducing vulnerability to sea-level rise. Some critics consider this fund too small; others see it not as an incentive to make CDM projects more development-friendly but as a tax on CDM investment.

Finally, realism about the role of national targets for reducing emissions is important. Many green supporters of Kyoto feel the treaty is useful because it legally binds governments to reduce emissions. But some governments – notoriously the USA under George Bush – have pulled out, ostensibly because the targets are not applied to all countries. Under Bill Clinton, the US had been central to negotiating targets that were too weak anyway, and the 'flexible mechanisms' that undermine measures to reduce emissions at source. Most importantly, rapidly industrialising countries such as China and India may well not agree to limit and reduce emissions.

Many companies and NGOs still entertain romantic visions of a carbon offset forestry replacing lost rainforests; and treat politically – rather than scientifically – agreed national targets as the only effective means to reduce emissions. But rather than idealising these, perhaps governments should impose targets for industry and consumers to seek a safe proportion of their energy from renewable sources, and to improve energy efficiency. Such targets would encourage innovation and new investment, which reduces the costs of safer technologies in the longer term. In a context of imminent (or recently passed) 'peak oil' production, a member of the UN Climate Change Secretariat noted privately that 'climate change is like god – if it did not exist, it would have to be invented'. This reflects the urgency of the shifts in energy policy and investment which the threat of climate change could, or should, be provoking.

Why should governments, supposedly working for the good of the people, perpetuate economic analysis and environmental policy that assume and play to the brutish, marketised and greedy side of our nature, and avoid the major changes needed to adapt our societies in the face of the depletion of finite resources? Where is the faith that humans can work together to adapt and seek more equitable solutions to collective problems?

Rather than devising 'solutions' to climate change that work only inside the very same market system that got us into this hole, a better approach may be to stop digging altogether. As a species we certainly have the ingenuity to make our governments adopt responses that do not impose new problems on poorer, less adaptable countries while maintaining big business' record profits. Rather, assisting all citizens to live more sustainable and comfortable lives would mean accepting that the debate about collective responses to the threat of climate change is not 'over', but still only just beginning.

Further information

http://www.tyndall.ac.uk/media/news/beyond_stern.s html http://www.carbontradewatch.org
http://www.sinkswatch.org
http://www.newgreenorder.info

Tim Forsyth <t.j.Forsyth@lse.ac.uk> is a writer and lecturer at the London School of Economics. He is author of International Investment and Climate Change, Earthscan, London, 1999

Zoe Young <zoe@esemplastic.net> is a freelance researcher, writer and filmmaker. She is author of A New Green Order? The World Bank and the Politics of the Global Environment Facility, Pluto, London, 2002

PROMISED LANDS

> It's not just the founders of hippy communes or artists like Amy Balkin who are looking for 'a breathing space from the State' in which to experiment with freedom and free-time. Big IT companies like Google apparently share their ideals. With a commitment to 'me time', the production of 'universal access', and (energy) sovereignty, corporates are leveraging the dream of the commons. **By Kate Rich**

Public Domain

This is the Public Domain is a real-estate undertaking by San Francisco artist Amy Balkin: the attempt to create a permanent, international commons on American soil, free to everyone in the world to access, use and modify, in perpetuity. Land shared by anyone who chooses to participate. In order to take this proposition off the high prairie of pure speculation and confront the infrastructural issues it raises head on, a piece of land was purchased by the artist in 2003. The land was visited, documented and, at the time of writing, is in holding for the legal process to transfer perpetual ownership to all humans. An ambitious task, strategies for which are published

Images of the Googleplex corporate campus in Mountain View, by Eros Hoagland. All images of Morningstar Ranch by anonymous hippies

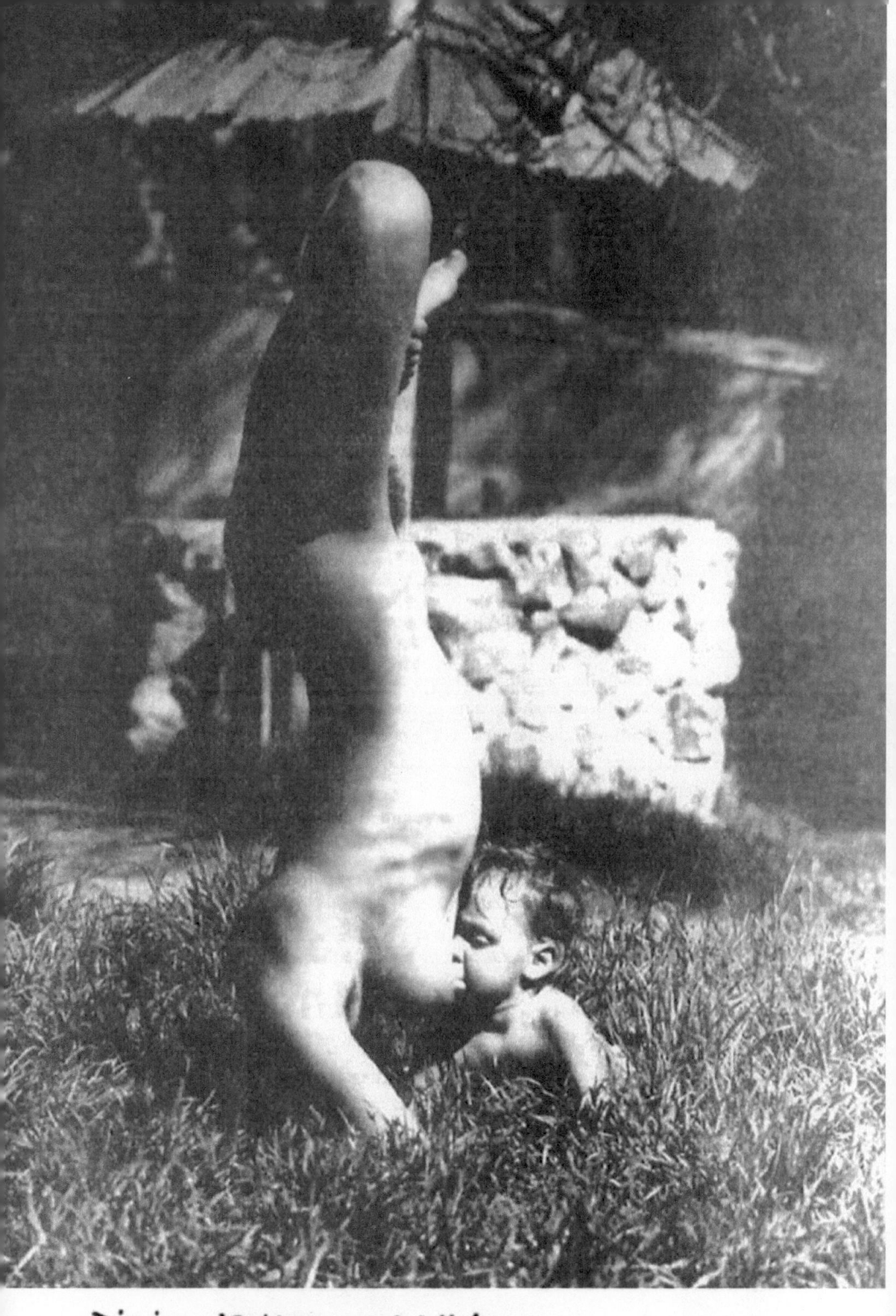

Divine Mother and Vishnu sucking tit.

on the project website [www.thisisthepublicdomain.org]. It is interesting to consider *Public Domain* in the light of a couple of other property developments that sprang from the fertile northern California soil.

Google Land

In 2006 Google, a California-based company, quietly went and bought a 35 acre chunk of former farmland in the Dalles, Oregon, an industrial and agricultural outpost 80 miles east of Portland. Google will not speak on record, but general understanding has it that the land will be used to site a data centre (server farm). Local amenities include various coffee houses and an array of recreational facilities such as kayaking in the cool Colorado River.

To trace the lovable search giant back to its roots, Google came to be in a landscape orientated around kinship networks, the close-knit corporate community of Silicon Valley, CA. The company was incorporated there in 1998 in the gift-ecology of a friend's garage in Menlo Park, out of whose humble dimensions it burst forth like Tetsuo to occupy its current HQ – the Googleplex corporate campus in nearby Mountain View.[1]

The Oregon acquisition sees Google expand into territory unlinked by kith or kin. The Dalles is previously only famed for the first 20th century bio-terrorist attack in the USA. In 1984 followers of the Bhagwan Shree Rajneesh cult attempted to control a local election by infecting 10 restaurant salad bars with salmonella and according to some sources locals from the area are famously hostile to incoming Californians. However, as well as the ample sporting opportunities to keep Google engineers tired yet happy, the location is noted for a steady excess of cheap, local electricity in the form of bulk-buy hydro-electric power from the town's own dam; and lashings of fibre optics brought to the area by a forward thinking councillor. Overall, a grounded ecological land move, indicating that in its attention to self-sustainability and energy security, Google may be well ahead of the pack.[2]

Just like Google, *Public Domain* found itself guided to land in a location which makes little sense in terms of neighbourliness. A limited acquisition budget (and staff) made for a purchase in landscape of least use-value and hence real-estate resistance. 2.5 acres in Antelope Valley in the California High Desert 125 miles east of Los Angeles was purchased by Balkin via public internet auction in 2003. The site can be seen as a pure distillation of land as commodity – the grid-like layout of property lines in the California desert clearly not attenuated to any coordinates of ecology or use, an artefact of pure speculation. The land is fully landlocked: no public roads access it, there are no

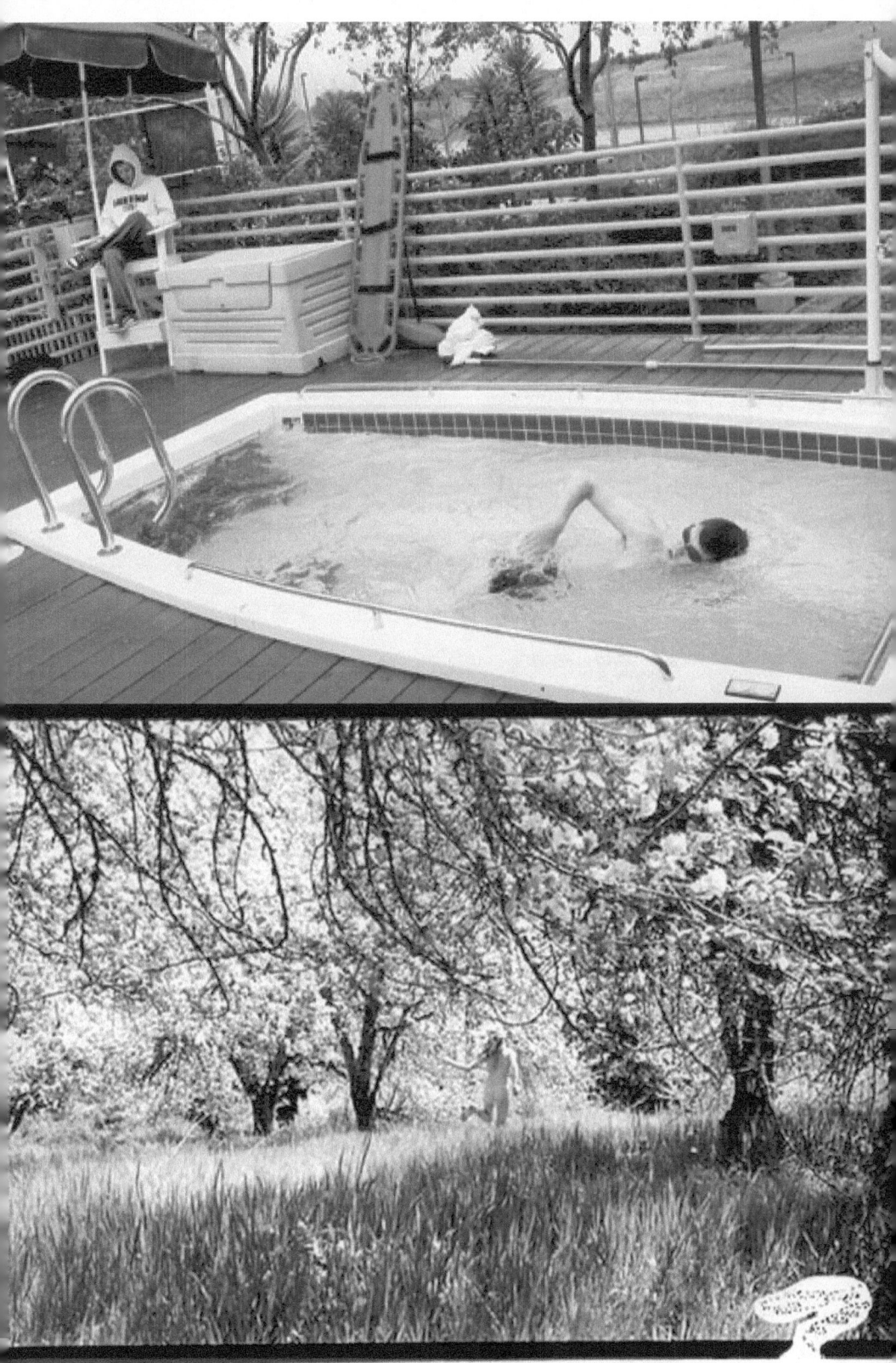

MORNING STAR ORCHARD IN April-blossom time.

antelopes, and its survivalist potential even on a day trip is minimal (low scrub, snakes, 40+ mph winds, desert temperatures, no water). The local sports opportunities are hard to interpret. However the point is not what the land has, but what it can act as.

Public Domain is conceived as 'breathing space from the state'. A place that you can't be hounded off of, like public parks where you often have to pay or there are drastic time and behavioural limits on use – for example, subsistence of any kind. It is ironic that this breathing space should, in this first attempt to materialise it, be functionally blocked by the Tehachapi wind farm (the world's second largest!) that surrounds the Public Domain land on all sides, in its awesome toil of commodifying the air's movements.[3] The concept of open land as refuge from the law was inspired in part by another Bay Area landholder, Morningstar Ranch.

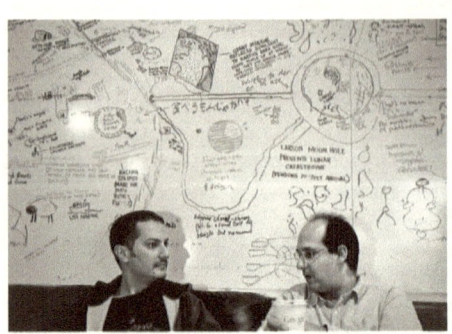

Open Land

Morningstar Ranch was established by comedian-academic Lou Gottlieb who set up a hippy commune in Marin County near San Francisco in the 1960s. In 1969, facing a state-ordered injunction against letting people live on his 31 acre holding, Gottlieb signed over the title of the property to God. When taken to court in 1971 for running an 'organised camp', he embarked on an attempted defence of his constitutional right to deed his land to God (which failed, although interestingly).[4] Lou Gottlieb described Morningstar as a pilot study in survival for a time when leisure is compulsory.

Google as Organised Camp

The affinities between Morningstar and Google are uncanny. Both emerged from the verdant San Franscisco hinterlands,

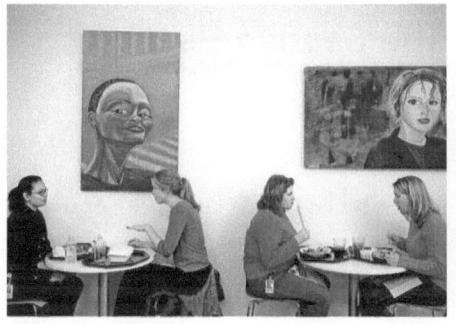
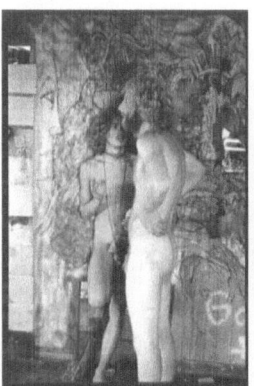
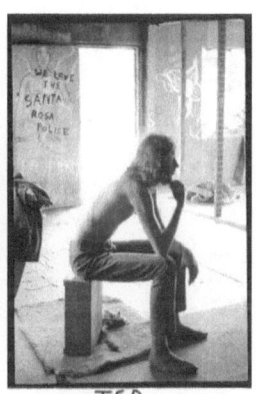

and are characterised by their experimental tendencies. At Google, a culture of campus fun reigns, with free snacks and 20 percent 'me time', in which all Google engineers are encouraged to spend 20 percent of their work time on projects that interest them, which interestingly seems to be inventing new Google products such as Gmail. It's not unlike the production ethos of free/libre and open source software (powered by social recognition and the curiosity for creation), although underwritten in Google's case by the heavy collateral of salaries, stock options,

Lou Gottlieb described Morningstar as a pilot study in survival for a time when leisure is compulsory

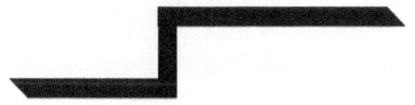

and an increasing amount of infrastructural resources.

Like many a California collective, Google's corporate philosophy is littered, throw pillow like, with many casual principles, for example, 'You can make money without doing evil.' Their Mountain View HQ is also decorated with lava lamps, exercise balls, washer-dryers, video games and snack rooms stocked with various cereals, yoghurt, gummy bears, toffees, cashews. Founder Larry Page said in an interview with *Playboy* magazine, 'We think a lot about how to maintain our culture and the fun elements, we think it's important to have a high density of people. People are packed together everywhere. We all share offices.' Google's 'about' page confirms this, adding that high-density offices is a great way to save on heating bills.

A search for more energy issues on Google Blog ('googler insights into product and technology news and our culture') reveals that Google is planning to install solar panels to decorate the outside of its Mountain View HQ; although a Google Blog search on the Dalles comes back empty. Home grown Dalles online chatter yields more background info, like that the combination of the Dalles Dam (a 1.8 million kilowatt generating facility), and the Columbia River's cooling capacity, has long attracted mega-energy users such as aluminium smelters to the region.

The Searing Heat of Data

In fact, Yahoo, Google, and Microsoft are all building new data centres in Oregon and Washington, near hydroelectric power plants selling cheap electricity. With the vast concentration of energy needed to run the megaservers – and equal and opposite megawattage needed to remove the excess heat – power and cooling have surfaced as critical issues in the expansion of global IT.[5]

On Blogger.com, another service owned and operated by Google, the typically taciturn search engine let slip, in March 2005, that 'New machines are not an issue because here at Google we can add them quite smoothly as needed. The real issue is power – actual electricity, if you can believe it'. Further delving finds the company browsing for more land in South Carolina: 520 acres purchased from the state electricity company at Goose Creek; 466 acres with their own electrical substations near Blythewood; 300 acres of wetlands close to a nuclear power station in Columbia. Perhaps Google is bunkering down for some kind of mini-apocalypse where power supply will be intermittent, parochial, fraught; but where being the world's search engine will still be super-lucrative and handy.

Something for Everyone

Google's mission statement is 'to organise the world's information and make it universally accessible and useful'.[6] Universal access and use is just what *Public Domain* has in mind. The artist has proposed a number of possible strategies to enact this, such as creating a public land trust to protect endangered forms of social space and donating the land to it (a real property law based strategy); or via a Public Domain Sharing Licence adapted from the Free Software Foundation's GNU GPL (a copyright law bending approach).[7] This license is designed to guarantee your freedom to share land (that you receive directions to the land, that you can occupy or modify the land) and forbids you to deny these rights to others.

In transplanting open source principles to the great outdoors, *Public Domain* highlights an action-gap of Evil Knievel proportions between current discourses around digital and material rights – in particular the broad non-transference of popular interest in implementing an information or knowledge commons, onto the more tufty surface of common ground.[8]

Transfer of protocols across the immaterial-material border can be tricky. Richard Stallman, author of the GNU GPL, claims to be against appropriation of the GPL for other things, insisting that the licence doesn't make sense beyond software.[9] Stallman argues that the GPL is based on copyright law and as physical objects don't have source code or copiers for them, the 'four freedoms' of free software (freedom of use; freedom to study how it works and adapt it; freedom to redistribute it; and freedom to make and publish improvements) don't apply. This raises rapid questions about 3D printers (which enable the automatic construction, reproduction and transmission of physical objects using solid freeform fabrication over data networks), and further the problem of securing software freedoms without acknowledging computer hardware. Without the same ferocity and community safeguarding the infrastructure and knowledge around material resources (circuits, minerals, electricity), the free software utopia might cease to have anything to run on.[10]

Back to the Land

At a recent panel discussion organised by Amy Balkin in San Francisco to explore how common land can be created and safeguarded, Ramon Sender, one of the original Morningstar ranchers and the custodian of its archives noted that emparkment (national parks) makes land public thereby criminalising communities who had derived their subsistence from it.[11] He positioned open land as a critique of private property and the extinction of use rights inherent in state-owned public land.[12]

Balkin herself found it more poignantly oppressive that the actual borders of the windfarm, while creating immediate physical and legal barriers to land access and use, are lesser impediments to total access and use than the physically more remote borders of the State. However to say that *Public Domain* will fail due to the world's people not having access to Antelope Valley is beside the point. To continue the analogy with free software, it is the *use* of free software (or open land) that activates the rights attached to it – the conditionality of *being there* is built-in.

Meanwhile, self-searching Google for more on Google Dalles, results bring up not a lot: one *New York Times* story from June 2006; a few derivative stories; and some others about being unable to file a story because Google wouldn't provide any information, and some blog chatter about all this. The most recent material is from the jobs section: 'Hardware Operations Team Manager – The Dalles. Solid understanding of supporting infrastructure for server and network gear, such as but not limited to, power and cooling requirements.' As well as, 'Technicians – The Dalles. Excellent understanding of Computer Room Air Conditioners (CRAC units), HVAC, Uninterruptible Power Supply (UPS), cooling and ventilating data, humidification/dehumidification, chillers' plus 'Temps with Linux knowledge, ability to work on ladders or under raised floor as needed and ability to lift/move up to 40 lbs equipment on a daily basis.'

Energy, Security and Space For All

Patri Friedman, a current Google employee, probably in his 'me time' writes of himself in his biog: 'Having investigated the various options, he's decided that floating cities are the most realistic path towards true liberty. He believes that sea and space will be conducive to liberty, and is writing a book about Seasteading, or homesteading the high seas.'[13] Although that idiot savant Hollywood has already captured all these libertarian, extra-terrestrial escapist themes in 2007's *Astronaut Farmer*, where another mad rancher Charles Farmer builds a rocket in his barn and intends to send himself into space. When he buys a bunch of rocket fuel, the FBI finds out and threatens a loan foreclosure on his ranch, Farmer fights back: 'if we don't have our dreams, we have nothing.' If Google can see the importance of sorting out the physical as well as the infrastructural, where does this leave the rest of us dreamers? Back on the ground, *Public Domain* continues its search for real-world frameworks to implement a legal solution for sharing the land. Juridicial expertise and precedents welcomed. 🖎

Footnotes

1
The Bureau of Inverse Technology's bit plane flew over and photographed this and many other seminal garages, including Hewlett Packard's birth garage, in its pioneering aerial sortie over Silicon Valley real estate in 1998. http://bureauit.org/plane

2
Although most of this is highly speculative, this reporter, not having the resources to physically get to Oregon, and with Google's policy of not answering questions, information is largely gathered from Google through searching on Google.

3
Commodifying the air is also of interest to Amy Balkin in her Public Smog project which constructs an international clean air park in the atmosphere via buying carbon offsets and retiring them from the emissions market, thereby making them inaccessible to polluting industries. http://www.publicsmog.org

4
The court case was recently re-encated in San Francisco from original transcripts, details at http://uo.twenteenthcentury.com/index.php/FacultyReenactment. More on Morningstar Ranch at http://www.diggers.org/home_free.htm

5
http://www.opensparc.net/news/2007-02/union-tribune-going-green-at-your-data-center-building.html Artist Heath Bunting's project Computer Dried Fruit deals with similar core issues.

6
Google founders Sergey Brin and Larry Page explain in a letter to Wall Street 'Searching and organizing all the world's information is an unusually important task that should be carried out by a company that is trustworthy and interested in the public good.'

7
A widely-used free software licence, more at http://www.gnu.org/copyleft/gpl.html

8
Eben Moglen, FSFs chief lawyer points out that the GNU GPL 'creates a contractual commons, to which anyone may add but from which no one may subtract.' Which neatly reverses the common land problem with endless legal variations for subtracting land from common ownership, but few means by which to restore it.
http://emoglen.law.columbia.edu/my_pubs/anarchism.html

9
Cube-Cola has been developing, modifying and distributing a physical cola drink from an open source recipe at the Cube Microplex Bristol, since 2004.
http://sparror.cubecinema.com/cube/cola

10
See HowStuffIsMade (a visual encyclopaedia that documents the manufacturing processes, labour conditions and environmental impacts involved in the production of contemporary products, [http://xdesign.ucsd.edu/howstuffismade]), Instructables.com (step-by-step instructions for making things you never knew you wanted, [http://www.instructables.com]), Materials & Applications (a research centre dedicated to pushing new and underused ideas for landscape and architecture into view, [http://www.emanate.org]) and NASA (we explore and discover, [http://www.nasa.gov]) for rare exceptions to the highly proprietary culture of fields such as industrial design, engineering and architecture.

11
This panel was part of the Wattis Institute's exhibition Radical Software, curated by Will Bradley, http://www.wattis.org/exhibitions/2006/software

12
http://www.raysender.com/morningstar.html

13
http://seastead.org

Thank you for sharing: research and advice from Amy Balkin, Jenna Didier, Oliver Hess, Lucia Sanroman and Josephine Berry Slater

Kate Rich <kate@bureauit.org> is an artist and trader, based in Bristol UK. She is currently developing amenities for hospitality, sports and survival in the cultural realm

APOCALYPSE AND/OR BUSINESS AS USUAL? THE ENERGY DEBATE AFTER THE 2004 US PRESIDENTIAL ELECTIONS

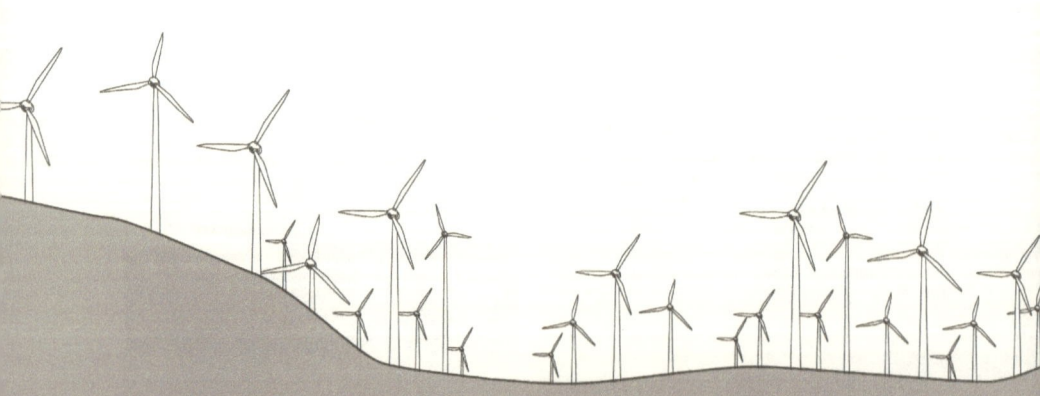

George Caffentzis

Since 2004 the rhetoric of Bush's republican party has turned curiously green, integrating climate change as a legitimation for neoliberal imperialism. At the same time the unintended consequence of America's unsuccessful adventures has been to enrich an 'anti-neoliberal' class of oil rentiers in Africa, Latin America and Asia.
George Caffentzis plots the changes in the US energy policy as it turns from eco-naysayer to ecowarrior

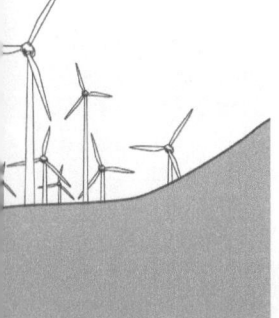

T he 2004 Presidential Election was in part a referendum on energy policy in the US. The Bush campaign expressed scepticism about both the Global Warming and Peak Oil hypotheses and claimed that the unleashing of the free market (including the lifting of some environmental restrictions) is the proper path for dealing with the energy problems of the US and the planet. In other words, there are no problems concerning energy that a dose of neoliberal privatisation and globalisation can't cure. The Bush 'Deal' with the US working class was that if workers supported his policies (including financing and staffing the required imperial military), the bulk of the costs of the new energy regime will be borne by the proletarians in the oil producing countries of Africa, Latin America and Asia. An important corollary to the 'Deal' was that there would be no need for a drastic wage decrease (caused by high oil prices) in the US.

It's Not Easy Being Green 53

Apocalypse and/or Business as Usual?

This was a call for the continuation of neoliberal business as usual. The Kerry campaigners took both Global Warming and Peak Oil seriously and proposed an approach to energy that would emphasise conservation and alternative energy production. Such policy, they claimed, would strengthen 'national security' without resort to war (the

what concerns Bush's class is a shortage of value, not a shortage of oil or natural gas

assumption being that if the US imported less oil, there would be fewer enticements to be drawn into 'resource wars' like the invasion of Iraq in the future). The Kerry 'Deal' being proffered to the US working class would require in exchange for 'national security' tolerance for high oil prices (to incentivise alternative energy production) and hence a dramatic reduction of the real wage in the US. It was a strident call to avoid an energy apocalypse. I criticised the Kerry campaign/ Democratic Party/ Environmentalist NGO position in a previous article in *Mute* (*Mute* Vol.1,

Issue 29, Winter/Spring 2005). In this article I will discuss some of the twists and turns of this energy debate among global capitalist 'deciders' since 2004 and the causes of these changes.

After the election, Bush continued to push ahead on the effort to increase oil drilling in the US (especially in the Arctic and the Gulf of Mexico) and to apply military pressure on oil producing nations to neoliberalise their oil industry, with Iraq being at the centre of the strategy. However, over the last two years there has been an evident change in the Bush Administration's rhetoric. In the 2006 State of the Union Address Bush unveiled his 'Alternative Energy Initiative' with these words: 'America is addicted to oil, which is often imported from unstable parts of the world.' In the 2007 State of the Union Address Bush held out hope that the research into new energy technologies his administration is supporting 'will help us confront the serious challenge of global climate change.' Neutral or even positive references to the reality of Global Warming and Peak Oil have begun to appear in official administration documents. This should not be surprising, if one looks at what has transpired in the last two and a half years concerning the class politics of global energy. The neoliberal effort, supported

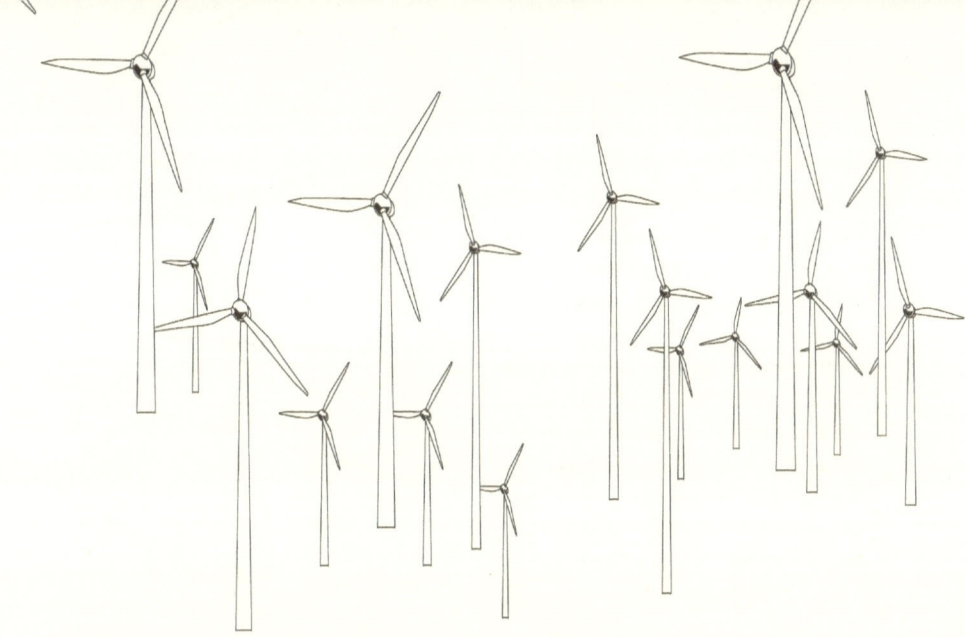

by the guns of the US military, to overturn the nationalisation of energy resources (especially oil and natural gas) has met reverses across the planet. Let me list a few of the more spectacular ones:

> – the failure of the US invasion of Iraq to impose a neoliberal regime on the nation's oil production;
> – the renationalisation of the natural gas industry of Bolivia;
> – the electoral triumphs of Chavez that have given his government the legitimation to use oil revenues to create a 'socialism for the 21st century' in Venezuela;
> – the successful 'stealth renationalisation' of the Russian oil industry by President Putin's government;
> – the oil companies' and Nigerian government's inability to crush the armed resistance of local Niger Delta groups demanding property rights in the oil reserves and reparation for past environmental damage.

This is not a pretty picture for the Bush Administration's neoliberal globalisation plan. When these reversals are summed up across Africa, Latin America and Asia, a remarkable phenomenon can be observed: the formation of a new 'rentier' class that is in opposition to neoliberalism. A rentier is someone who lives off rents and returns from investments, in other words, someone whose revenue arises from the transfer of surplus value from other parts of the capitalist system. In early modern Europe, the landed rentier class was made up of aristocratic families that rented out their land to capitalist farmers. The problematic part of the contemporary oil rentier class is made up of governments (e.g., mullah-ruled Iran, '21st century socialist' Venezuela) and ethnic organisations (the U'wa of Colombia, the Ijaw of the Niger Delta, and the indigenous West Papuans) that are demanding the right to use the rents and transferred surplus value they receive (or ought to receive) in a non-, or even an anti-capitalist manner (to the point that the U'wa would ban all drilling into the flesh of mother earth!).

Across Africa, Latin America and Asia, a remarkable phenomenon can be observed: the formation of a new anti-neoliberal 'rentier' class

This part of the oil rentier class worries the Bush Administration more than the apocalyptic scenarios Peak Oil

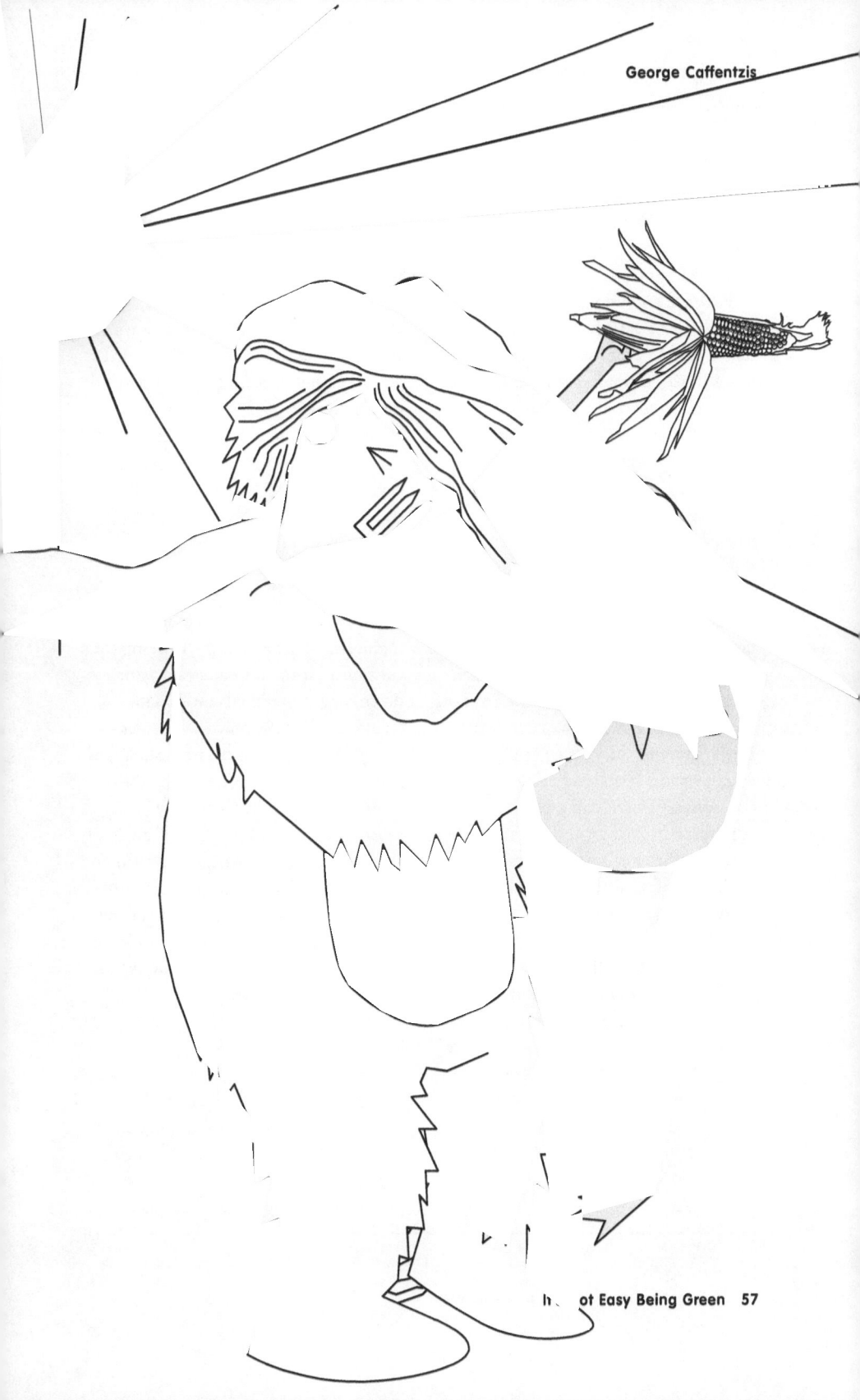

and Global Warming activists delight in telling. In fact, much of the Bush Administration's newly found attraction to Peak Oil and Global Warming is part of the effort to justify the failure to deliver on the promises of cheaper oil and a threat to troublesome oil rentiers. For after all, there are only two major threats that can be used against the rentiers: (a) direct military force threatening to dispossess them of their resources; (b) the development of alternative non- oil/natural gas energy sources threatening to devalue their resources. The failure of the Iraq invasion to lead to either increased oil production or even a legal change opening up the oil industry to foreign company control has shown the limits of the military effort. Consequently, the Bush Administration, even as it continues to surge ahead in its occupation of Iraq (and threatens to bomb Iran in the bargain), must develop the other threat so openly described by the Saudi oil minister, Sheik Ahmed Zaki Yamani in 1981:

> If we force the Western countries to invest heavily in finding alternative energy sources, they will. This will take them no more than seven to ten years and will result in their reduced dependence on oil as a source of energy to a point which will jeopardise Saudi Arabia's interests.

Capitalist concern over the anomalous behaviour of the landlord or rentier class is not new. Rentiers affect the struggle between capitalists and workers in complex and often problematic ways. In Britain, for example, the rentiers sided with the capitalists for the most part during the rise of capitalism (with occasional violent falling outs in the 17th century). But by the 18th century, capitalist thinkers were debating the negative consequences of 'absentee' landlords' 'luxury' consumption and by the early 19th century political economists like David Ricardo argued that rents reduced profits because of the high price of grain that the working class consumed. If the price of grain went down, wages would fall and profits would rise. But the only way for this to occur was to open up the importation of grain by reducing or eliminating the tariff on cereals. The Corn Law (so called because in England 'corn' refers to any 'cereal grain') legislated this tariff and so Ricardo called for its repeal. He urged his fellow capitalists to end their alliance with the rentiers, since the flourishing of the latter would threaten the survival of the former. Ever since this period, 'rentier' became a synonym in economics for a lazy, obstreperous and parasitic being. 'Rent', when it was not the object of opprobrium, was barely mentioned in the economics text books. But like it or not, rents and rentiers have played an important role in capitalism down to the present, especially in the oil industry.

The oil industry also has another kind of transferred surplus value besides rent that arises because oil production is technology intensive and almost labour-less. Hence the oil industry creates very little surplus value. On the other side, the oil industry is quite profitable. Where does this profit come from? It arises from other parts of the system that create much surplus value while requiring relatively little technological investment. This leads to the owners of the oil companies receiving transferred value and if these owners are landlords who own the oil resources as well, they can receive two kinds of income.

Until the early 1970s the oil rentiers (the recipients of both these transfers of value) were relatively amenable to capital's desires, but since then and especially in the last couple of years many rentiers have become dangerous to the neoliberal accumulation of capital. The most visible example is the political movement that brought Hugo Chavez to presidential power in Venezuela, of course, but there are many other actual political and social movements that are rejecting the neoliberal claim that the best way to maximise everyone's utility is to denationalise the oil industry and return it to the hands of the global energy companies. In fact, they are using oil revenues to increase wages and invest in the reproduction of workers. For example, the Chavez administration is financing a major land redistribution drive to benefit the slum dwellers of Caracas using the oil revenues.

The true worry of the Bush Administration is that these troublesome oil rentiers will unite with each other and form an alliance with the working classes of their territory that will harm the exploitation of workers across the planet. After all, what concerns Bush's class is a shortage of value, not a shortage of oil or natural gas. Workers should be politically concerned by 'Peak Oil' scarcities and by 'Global Warming' apocalypses, but we must remember that capital is not. Scarcity and apocalypse are capitalist business as usual. In capital's history thousands of scarcities have been created in order to impose work and make a profit. It has destroyed ecologies and human populations time and again to preserve and extend its rule. What we should be concerned about is that this new turn in the class struggle that brings together working classes in Latin America, Africa and Asia with rentier governments and ethnic organisations in the oil producing regions will be attacked using 'Peak Oil' or 'Global Warming' as an ideological cover in the same way that nuclear non-proliferation has been used to invade Iraq.

George Caffentzis
<caffentz@usm.maine.edu> is a member of the Midnight Notes Collective and a co-ordinator of the Committee of Academic Freedom in Africa

John Jordan and James Marriot's operatic audio tour set in London's Square Mile is intended to awaken city workers to the impact of financial systems on climate change. But not only does *And While London Burns* misgauge how much the suits already know, its hysterical tone also harmonises too easily with the coming new eco-order. Review by <u>Anthony Iles</u>

HEAVY OPERA

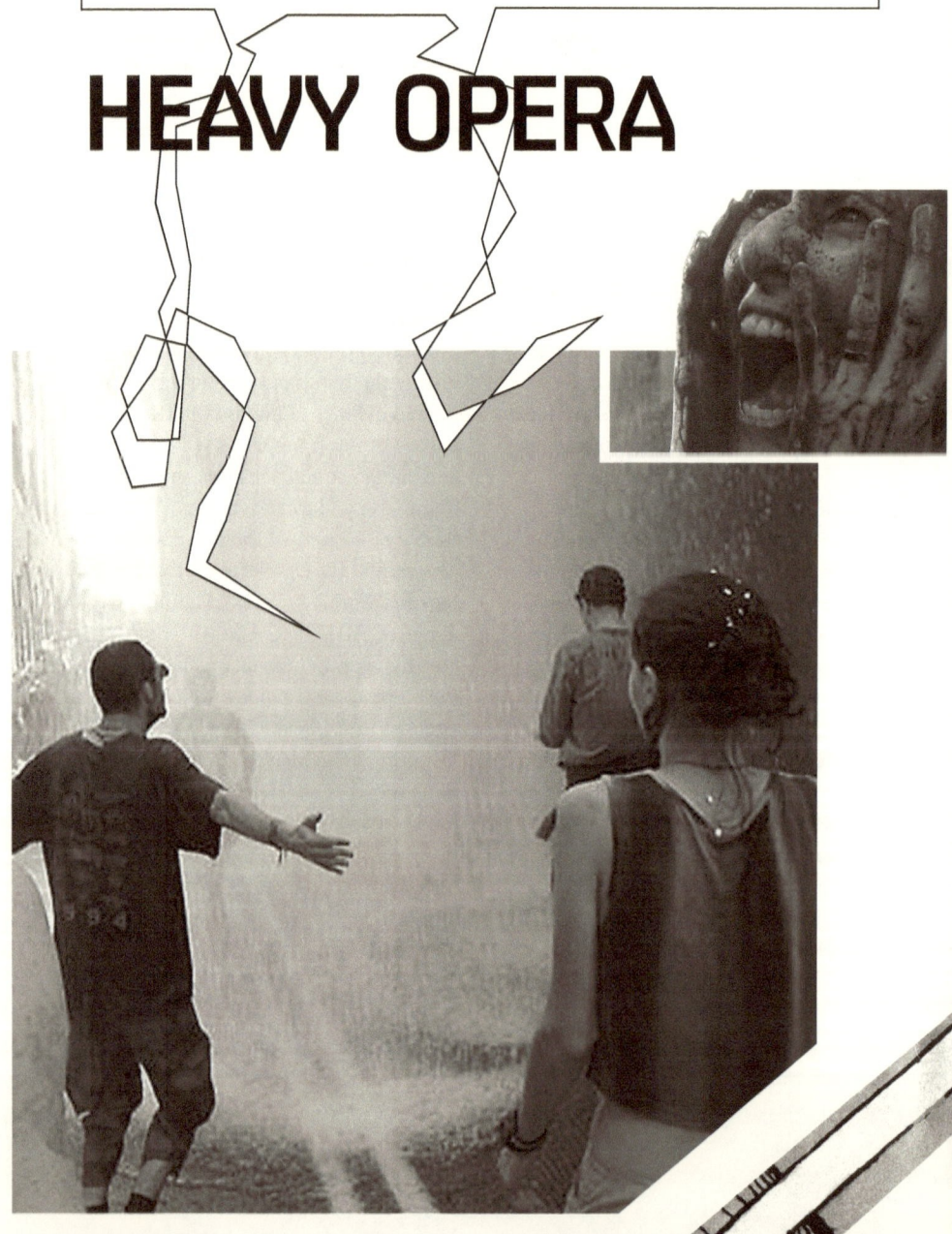

Anthony Iles

A fountain of water from the river Walbrook shoots up above my head, drums are pounding, a sound system's bass rumbles. I hear cheers but I can also hear the clatter of police shields and batons around the corner. Seven years after London's Carnival Against Capital, when protesters outside the LIFFE exchange broke a water mains sending a thirty-foot jet of water into the air, I am walking just a half a mile north of the same spot. Now I can hear the Thames rushing up the valley the Walbrook follows, bursting its banks, laying waste to the tall glass-fronted buildings as some of the most expensive real estate in London collapses around me. I'm swept up in a sonically induced fantasy driven by the tracks on my MP3player. I am taking part in *And While London Burns*, an operatic guided walk written by John Jordan and James Marriot, set to music by Isa Suarez and produced by the cross-disciplinary art and education group Platform.[1]

John Jordan has played a role in both these participatory dramas, firstly as a member of Reclaim the Streets – one of the anti-capitalist groups that coordinated the Carnival Against Capital in June 1999. This time around as an artist commissioned by Platform – an interdisciplinary arts, campaigning and research group committed to longer term, less partisan approaches to transforming the activities of the financial institutions and corporations with head offices in the Square Mile. The walk is an attempt to dramatise the research Platform has conducted into climate change. James Marriot, its co-founder, explains:

> 'It's a way of dramatising and humanising these systems [the role of multinationals

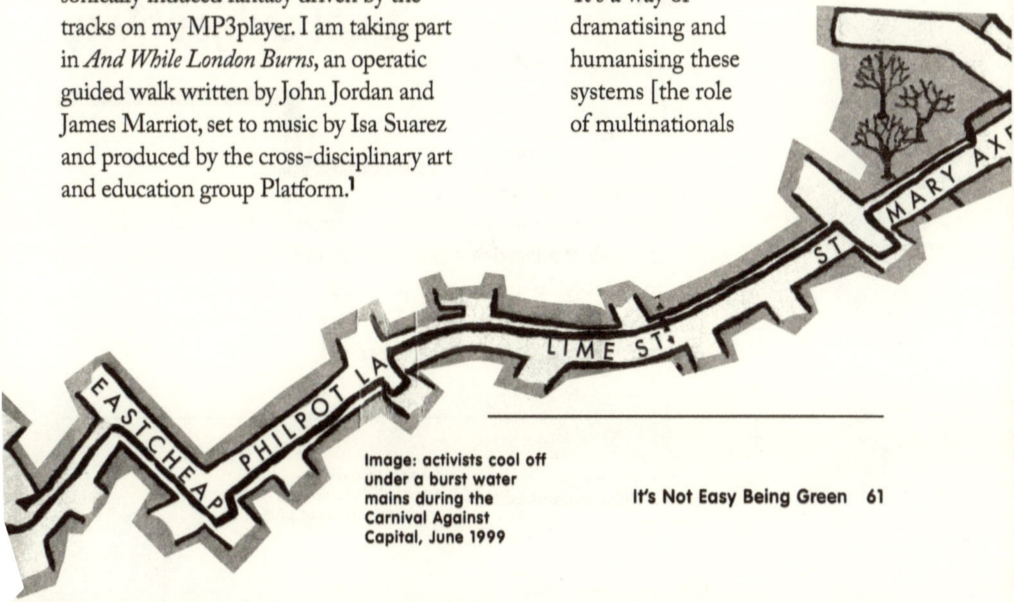

Image: activists cool off under a burst water mains during the Carnival Against Capital, June 1999

It's Not Easy Being Green 61

Heavy Opera

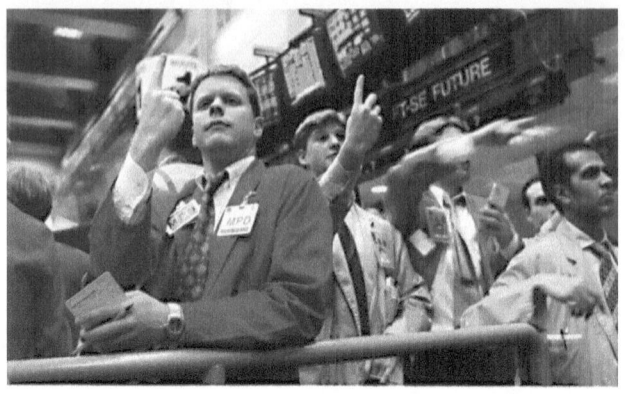

and financial systems in fuelling climate change]. It's over-dramatised like all opera, which is why we chose the medium.'**2**

The walk begins at 1 Poultry. At a Starbucks opposite the ruins of the Roman Temple of Mithras our attention is drawn to the multinational's logo with its allusions to paganism and older gods. The audio tour's protagonist remembers that before Starbucks went global its logo (designed after a 15th century print by Seattle hippy entrepreneurs) bore nipples and 'a pair of provocatively spread fishtails'. The mermaid allegorises both allegiance to, and fear of, the sea. She is exotic and, like the valuable cargoes on which the City's wealth was originally founded, unattainable for those doing the shipping. The City is still resplendent with powerful iconography from the 18th and 19th centuries, pineapples

> **The work engenders the opposite of an active, critical subjectivity**

and other exotic objects appear frequently as architectural ornaments advertising the City's plunder. Today, retail spaces and spaceship architecture adorned with surveillance cameras predominate. At the Royal Exchange (now a luxury shopping mall) our protagonist remembers:

Image: traders on London's Futures exchange in times past

Anthony Iles

I used to work here in 1989, when it was the Futures Exchange ... the place was a permanent carnival, traders in bright coloured jackets shouting and gesturing to each other ... it couldn't be more different now.

The new City outwardly tells little about where it draws value from and it is this occultation of money the walk confronts by whispering its secrets in your ear.

As its website explains:

> For over 20 years, PLATFORM has been bringing together environmentalists, artists, human rights campaigners, educationalists and community activists to create innovative projects driven by the need for social and environmental justice.[3]

Platform has gone some way beyond the statements required to declare oneself a corporate entity in the art world. Operating more like an NGO, Platform sought autonomy from the dependencies of art, eschewing support from established galleries or art spaces. Instead the group concentrates upon building relationships between environmentalists, artists and employees of the core financial and carbon-extracting institutions which, at the same time, are the objects of their research and criticism. Since art has taken a relational turn, Platform's dialogic practice has been somewhat vindicated and is gaining the interest of institutions with a commitment to engaging with 'public issues' outside the institutional safety zone.[4] The group has often employed organised walks, 'walking as a research tool, as a ritual, as performance, as intervention, as a political tool'.[5] Here, in the Square Mile that demarcated the original Roman settlement of Londinium, Platform taps the rich network of influence and accumulation they call the 'carbon web' – 'the web of institutions that extract oil and gas from the ground'.

Walking, I am accompanied by three voices or groups of voices. The protagonist, a disillusioned City worker, drifts, trying to throw off the pressure and hypocrisy of the city in an anguished monologue. The guide, a softly spoken, reassuring female voice, tells me when to cross, to 'be careful', 'look left and right at the lights', as well as offering information about BP, the financial groups and investors who support it (Morely, Deutsche Bank, Royal Bank of Scotland). The third voice is a chorus which echoes the protagonist's monologue and riffs eccentrically on it, singing 'They stole her nipples', 'look up,

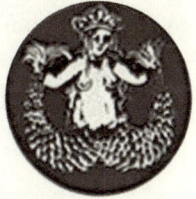

Image: the original Starbucks logo

Heavy Opera

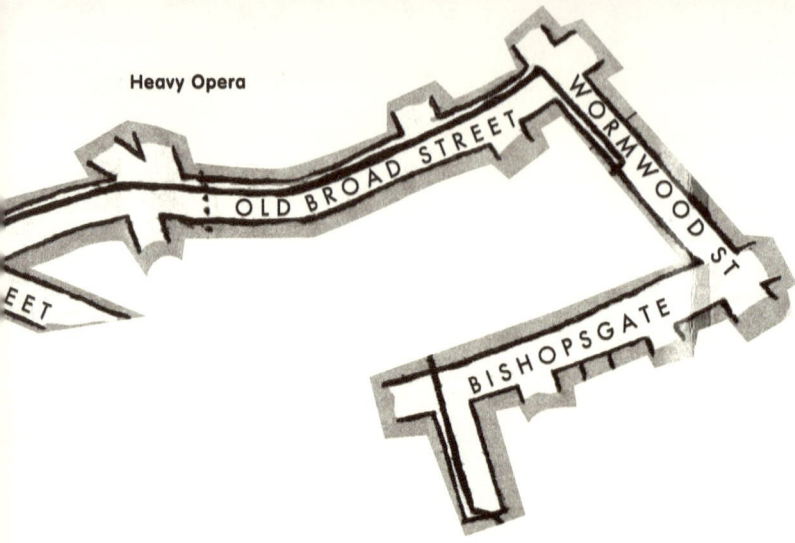

look up to the sky', and, in the Royal Exchange, chants: 'More, more and more, give us more money, give us more and more ...'.

The carefully guided walk sometimes becomes a gallop as I realise I have taken a wrong turn or when the voices urge me to speed up. As I am led under and through the City's architectural machines of accumulation, the opera emphasises its status as a principal node processing the world's financial flows. Later, I am spun around Bank station and the Swiss Re tower as the chorus and music builds to a crescendo prefiguring a portentous end to the narrative and the walk.

The accompanying music first appears to me as corporate muzak, like the sound of distilled comfort and class played as one waits for the bank's outsourced operatives to process your phone call. Later, the strings dramatise my rush around the city while street noise blends in as I lurch across streams of commuters and traffic. Once I accept that my route is programmed, I find myself caught up in what feels like the soundtrack to a live video game, gleefully aware that no-one else is conscious of my directed path.

And While London Burns is really an 'experience' – in the sense that a trip to Disneyland is. The walk deploys four dramatic elements: the narrative of personal crisis; the music; the information about the Earth's decline under capitalism; and the sounds and sights of the City itself. As the slew of information about the Earth's rising temperature builds to a picture of crisis, the protagonist becomes more erratic – we supposedly take on the burden of his self-realisation as our own. But then our 'own' crisis over climate change's destructive potential is experienced as adventure.

And While London Burns shares this array of simple mechanisms for dramatising the present really impending apocalypse with two recent films, *Apocalypto* and *Children of Men*. The latter plays out anarchist fantasies of a biopolitical neofascist state in the UK, presenting us with:

Anthony Iles

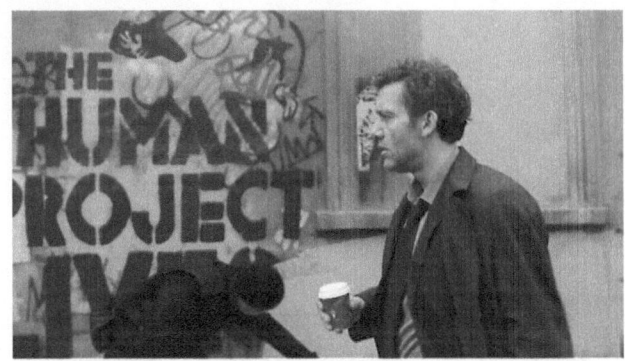

Image: still from
Children of Men

And While London Burns is really an 'experience' — in the sense that a trip to Disneyland is

a world one generation from now that has fallen into anarchy on the heels of an infertility defect in the population ... Set against a backdrop of London torn apart by violence and warring nationalistic sects, *Children of Men* follows disillusioned bureaucrat Theo (Clive Owen) as he becomes an unlikely champion of Earth's survival. **6**

Mel Gibson's *Apocalypto* draws a clumsy comparison between the internal breakdown of Mayan civilisation prior to Cortez's conquest of their lands and the demise of the US as a global hegemon:

Throughout history, precursors to the fall of a civilisation have always been the same .... It was important for me to make that parallel because you see these cycles repeating themselves over and over again. People think that modern man is so enlightened but we're susceptible to the same forces – and we are also capable of the same heroism and transcendence.**7**

These films, like with *And While London Burns*, indulge a reactionary millenarianism apparently appropriate to our times characterised by anxiety over reproduction, environmental devastation, migration and wars over resources. Each locates a subjective response to 'objective conditions' in a male subject, and we see an awakening to the real conditions of the societies in which they live.

For *And While London Burns'* authors one gets the feeling that it is something of a stretch of the imagination to place themselves in this character's shoes, that some under estimation of the ignorant and complacent 'suit' is operating. The dynamic between the identification of the listener with this disaffected conservative and the more 'radical imagination' celebrated through historical references was, for me, unconvincing.

I struggle with the opera's construction of experience (the listener's as well as the conditions they 'objectively' face) as consensus reality without challenge. It seems that after so long working at the margins of artistic practice, Platform have finally conceded to the monoform. There is no

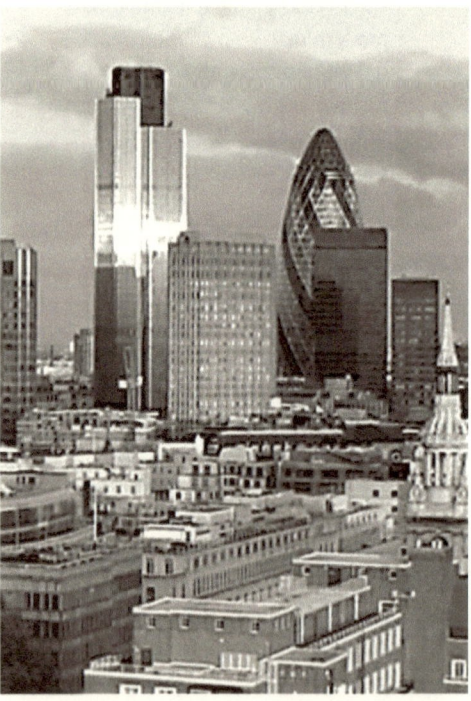

transcendental subject, no lone saviour of civilisation. Although *And While London Burns*' authors are the first to admit that they are self-consciously playing with clichés to dramatic effect, this walk is the very opposite of psychogeographic practice.[8] The work engenders the opposite of an active, critical subjectivity.

If there is a dialectic to be found in *And While London Burns* it is that of flight versus contestation. The audio guide points to the irony of the City as both a centre of research into the causes and effects of climate change (in particular Swiss Re, whose reinsurance business is predicated upon the mediation of threats to profitability) and the self-satisfied ignorance of continued irresponsible plunder. As the opera's story unravels we are informed that the protagonist's partner, Lucy, has left to live 'off-grid'. This response to the threat of environmental devastation is the conceptual equivalent of self-organising nuclear bunker drills at the height of the cold war – a duck and cover strategy, internalising the nuclear state's imperative that we be afraid, that we submit to pointless rituals in the face of death. At the opposite pole, the rich shoring up their wealth and access to unadulterated leisure and consumption in Dubai are playing a similar end-game with equally futile consequences. As if, in the context of a global emergency, anyone will be safe in either a low impact woodland home with its own energy supply or in a glass tower surrounded by the best defenses petro-dollars can buy. Both visions indulge in the fantasy that in the globalised world there is some escape or autonomy, a form of denial which hopes to obscure all ties between that secure haven and the reality of ongoing surplus value extraction from a landless, illegalised, starving (sub-) humanity.

And While London Burns puts this contemporary meme of millennial conservatism to work in a locale that is synonymous with unsustainable economics, personal debt and risk-taking. The work chooses to reinforce the personalisation and internalisation of a crisis for which capitalism itself should be paying the costs. Its dramatisation of the Earth's climactic instability hinges on a predicted four degree rise in temperature that we are now almost certain to reach according to the IPCC's recent report. The facts relayed during the course of this walk tend to confirm these projections. I am not in a position to challenge these facts. Without even trying to challenge these facts, it is still possible to object to the terms in which the urgency of change is being framed. The injunction of climate change is literally 'change'; through crisis, capital is reorganising itself and this has immediate social impacts. What is being proposed is a series of small adjustments for capital and many dramatic shocks for us. There appears to be very little going on in terms of large projects to actually reverse this situation,

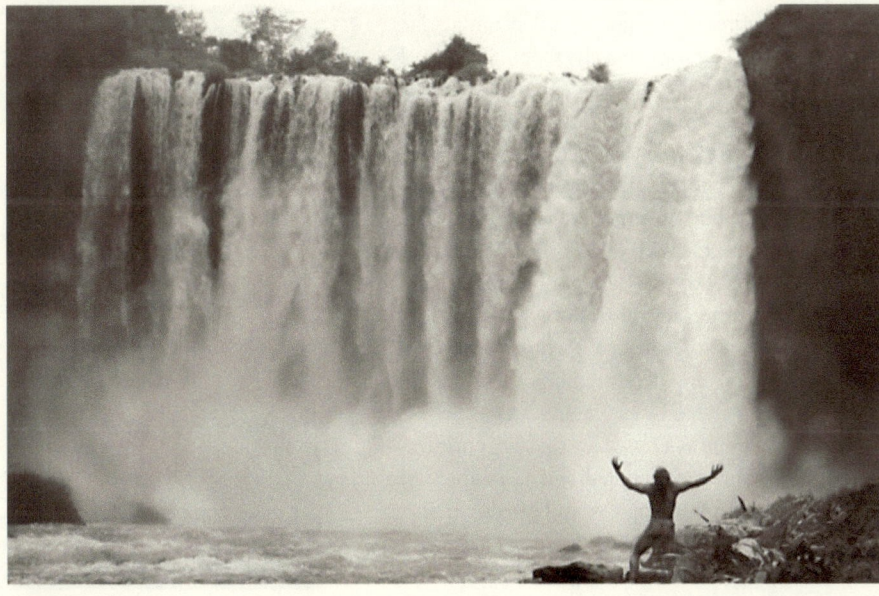

Image: still from *Apocalypto*

Heavy Opera

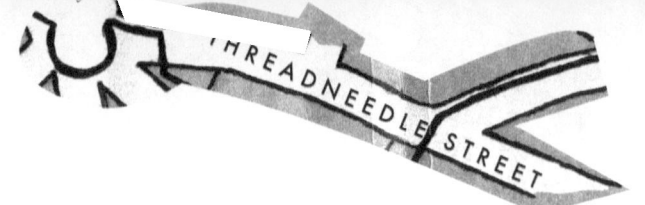

instead there is a confluence of self-righteous self-flagellation at a consumer level and government programmes to bully workers, small to medium-sized businesses and new home owners.

Platform have a background of deeper engagement with these issues and access to research that should allow them to analyse the joined up system of capitalist 'wealth creation' and its affect on the social environment. However, as the UK and other governments worldwide absorb green and environmental discourse and re-spin it as command – to eat less, work more, pay extra for energy and waste – some engagement with this instrumentalisation of ecological threat would be useful, rather than continuing to pursue an alarmist politics fuelling the fires of eco-fascism in becoming.

From apocalyptic predictions of dramatic climate change down to fashion tips for the greening of lifestyles, we experience exactly the same 'terrorism of conformity that underlies all the publicity of modern capitalism'.[9] The trouble with this work and almost all public discussion of climate, is that rather than critically evaluating the role of this ecological threat as part of the ongoing deterioration of living standards dictated by capital in most of the world, there is a tendency to exaggerate the threat, to rationalise it as a natural fact, and thus approve and provide training for the modification of behavior urged by capitalism.

Footnotes

1
Available for download at: http://www.andwhilelondonburns.com/download/

2
Anna Minton, 'Down to a Fine Art', *The Guardian*, 10 January

3
Platform website, http://www.platformlondon.org/aboutplatform.asp

4
Anna Minton, op. cit.. This celebratory piece highlights a new movement of artists fusing post-conceptual art and environmental art under the aegis of the Royal Society of Arts whose director, Matthew Taylor, was formerly head of the Prime Minister's policy unit. It would seem that relational aesthetics is rapidly emerging as the idiom by which artists speak to policy makers on behalf of the public.

5
Platform website, op. cit..

6
Children of Men website, http://www.childrenofmen.net

7
Mel Gibson on *Apocalypto* from the film website, http://apocalypto.movies.go.com

8
As one definition would have it: 'The theory of the combined use of arts and techniques for the integral construction of a milieu in dynamic relation with experiments in behavior'. Situationist International, 'Preliminary Problems in Constructing a Situation' in Ken Knabb, *Situationist International Anthology*, Bureau of Public Secrets, http://www.bopsecrets.org/SI/1.situations.htm

9
'Geopolitics of Hibernation', *Situationist International* #7, April 1962, http://www.bopsecrets.org/SI/7.hibernation.htm

Anthony Iles <anthony@metamute.org> is a writer and contributing editor of *Mute*

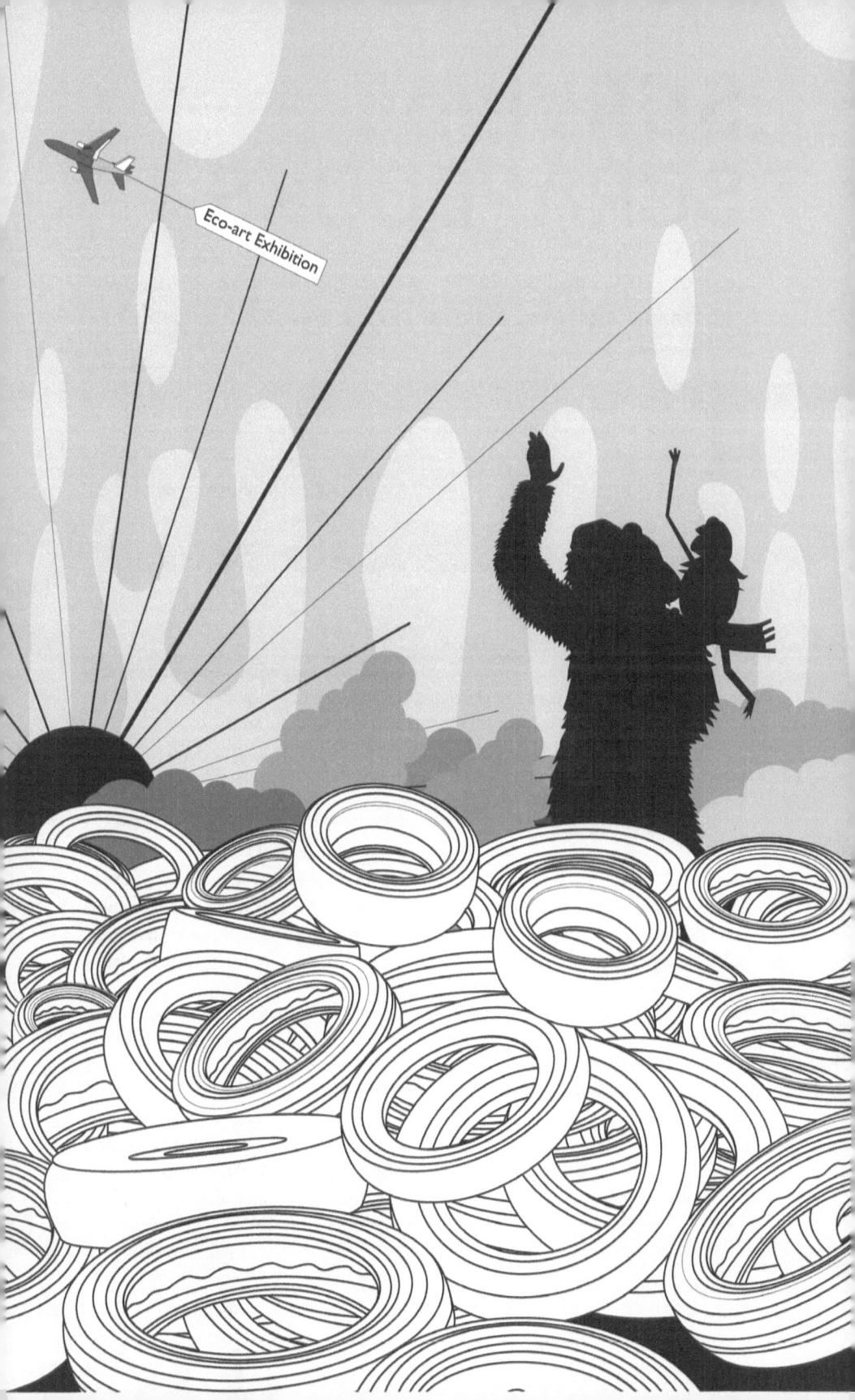

SURVIVAL SCRAPBOOKS

Simon Yuill unpacks 1970s radical culture through Stefan Szczelkun's seminal Survival Scrapbooks

The Survival Scrapbooks are a series of six books published in the early-1970s covering different aspects of autonomous living from a practical perspective. Several authors contributed to the series, often with additional input from others. The titles in the series, and their authors, were:

volume 1: *Shelter*, 1972 - Stefan Szczelkun
contents: different forms of wild, mobile, or simple-to-build accommodation including caves, hand-made tents, wooden huts, and vans.

volume 2: *Food*, 1972 - Stefan Szczelkun
contents: ways of harvesting rainwater, small-scale farming, poaching, growing mushrooms, as well as advice on nutrients and different forms of diet, and fresh air as food.

volume 3: *Access to Tools*, 1973 - Dave Williams and Stephanie Munro
contents: a directory of books, resources, organisations and where to buy tools for farming, building, publishing etc. Each entry includes some small example of useful information to illustrate it.

volume 3 1/2: *Play: Ways and Means*, 1973 - Pauline Vincent and Ann Winn
contents: different play and self-made learning activities 'for kids, parents, teachers, anybody'. These include textile and paper making but also recycling junk, basic photography and electronics and, according to the subject listing, the 'mastery of elegant insults'.

volume 4: *Paper Houses*, 1974 - Roger Sheppard, Richard Threadgill, and John Holmes
contents: a detailed instruction guide to building geodesic domes from paper and cardboard, including how to make the paper.

volume 5: *Energy* - Stefan Szczelkun
contents: various DIY energy systems such as wind turbines, waterwheels, bio-gas, and home-built solar panels, but also a section on psychic energies. Includes maps of naturally available energy sources (such as wind, water, wood) in Britain and the States.

The books were published by the Unicorn Bookshop in Brighton, with some titles re-printed in the States by Shocken. It started as an ongoing project and other titles were planned, such as one on squatting, one on communications and publishing, and one called 'Cracks in the Earth' on what to do when 'attacked by teenage vampires from Outer Space' amongst other things.

The styles of the different authors vary, as do the format of the books. Szczelkun's titles were all published with punch-holes in the pages so they could be removed from their cover and combined with other material in a ring-binder. The sections are each printed in a different coloured ink (purple, blue, red, brown, orange, etc) with a coloured strip and graphic icon in each outer edge to make it easy to flick through and find stuff. The texts are hand-written and a variety of different visual styles are used in the illustrations, including drawings by Clifford Harper, photographs, Victorian etchings and newspaper clippings. *Access To Tools* follows the format of the *Whole Earth Catalogue*, lots of compact boxes of information on each page a bit like the classified adds in a newspaper. This also has page-holes for a ring-binder. The other two books depart from this. *Paper Houses* is more like a conventional instruction manual with step-by-step diagrams and photographs, whilst *Play* is printed in landscape format typical of school activity-books at that time, although it is also the most visually intense with tons of drawings, photographs and pasted texts cramming the pages.

The scrapbook idea and ring-binder format utilises a particular form of information system that has a loose structure, and is intended to be re-edited. As such it is typical of many of the experiments with the book format that were explored in its day, and which led towards some of the structures that now characterise online publication, such as the Wiki. Classic examples of such texts are Ted Nelson's *Computer Lib* (1974 and 1975), Marvin Minsky's *Society of Mind* (from early 1970's onwards), and the *Whole Earth Catalogue* (1968 - 1998). Whilst volume 3, *Access to Tools* is clearly a British version of the *Whole Earth Catalogue* - it's title is the slogan from the *Catalogue*'s cover - there is also a shared set of themes between the *Catalogue* and the Scrapbooks as a whole: both share a strong influence of Buckminster Fuller's ideas, evident in themes such as knowledge as a tool, social-ecological systems, shelter, energy, and geodesic domes. In this sense they are equivalent US and British statements of early-1970's counterculture and alternative living. They differ in that most of the Scrapbooks provide more detailed explorations of particular topics, rather than general compendiums of knowledge. They also differ in terms of their textual archaeologies.

The *Whole Earth Catalogue* occupies a strata resting on 1960's radicalism, cybernetics and the emergence of the modern ecological movements, and is then layered-over by the rise of digital culture and the internet. The Survival Scrapbooks share much of this, but are also mixed in with fragments and shards of other discourses. The three books that Szczelkun worked on grew out of a period of living nomadically in a van (advice on which is given in volume 1: *Shelter*). Prior to this he had been involved in several collective projects, beginning with a version of Jim Haynes' Art Lab that he initiated whilst studying architecture at Portsmouth Polytechnic, followed by the Scratch Orchestra in London, and then the EarthWorkshop in Wales which accompanied his work on the Scrapbooks. Later, he went on to be involved in squatting and self-build projects in London, the Brixton Artist's Collective, Mail Art projects, set up Working Press, which published early texts by Matthew Fuller and Graham Harwood amongst others, and was part of the Exploding Cinema group.[1] Pauline Vincent and Ann Winn, authors of volume *3 1/2: Play*, were members of the Froebel Institute, an institute for training teachers based on the theories of Friedrich Froebel who was an early proponent of learning through play and activity, in which knowledge is a tactile experience.[2] This principle of learning through doing, of knowledge through

> titles were planned on what to do when 'attacked by teenage vampires from Outer Space' amongst other things

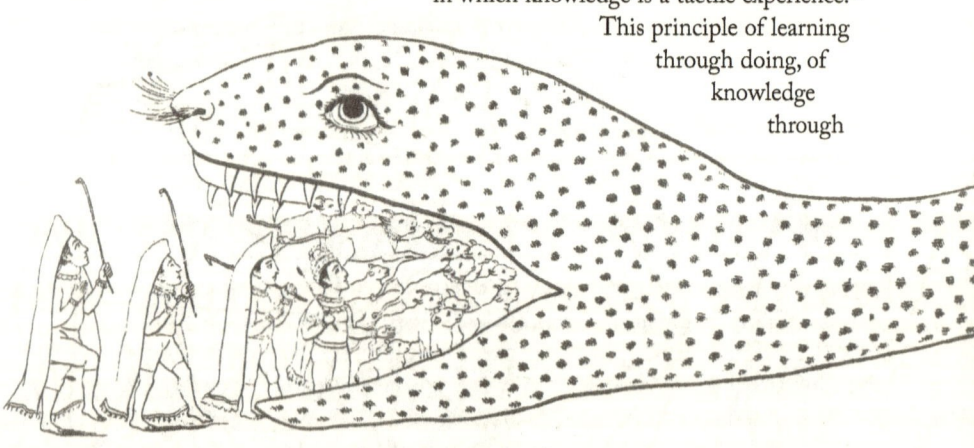

Image: Radical housing alternatives from *Survival Scrapbook Volume 1: Shelter*

action, is at the forefront of the Scrapbooks. Whereas the *Whole Earth Catalogue* provided a 'store' of knowledge tools, the Survival Scrapbooks are perhaps more a set of knowledge practices, ones which involve making your own tools:

> After you have changed it and made it work for your needs; GET OUT; make yourself a reality. Then tell everybody else about how you did it.**3**

The Survival Scrapbooks present a form of distributive practice. A distributive practice can be understood as a 'way of doing' that seeks to propagate the knowledge and resources through which it is generated, and which itself also generates, so that others may adopt and adapt it. The principle of distributiveness entails that the practice should be self-legitimating, adoption of the practice should not be dependent on passing tests, acquiring certification or the approval of governing bodies. A distributive practice is not a doctrine or discipline, with a set of canonical principles to be adhered to, nor does it require institutional representation, such as an academic qualification, martial art, or religious practice might. It allows for unplanned future mutations and re-inventions rather than seeking to guard against them.

The Scratch Orchestra was a group formed around the composers Cornelius Cardew, Michael Parsons and Howard Skempton in 1969. It became a platform in which a diverse range of people from various backgrounds, including trained musicians, artists and those outside of institutional arts, explored forms of collective improvisational music and performance. One of the main activities of the Orchestra were the creation of Scratch-books. Each member of the Orchestra kept their own Scratch-book which could be any kind of book (jotter, notebook, one member used a copy of the *Radio Times*) in which they produced their own experimental scores for performances - known as Scratch Music. The Scratch-books were representative of the general interest in new forms of musical notation that many composers were exploring in that time. Composers, such as John Cage, were trying to create forms of music that could not be expressed by conventional Western notation and so had turned to developing new notational systems to compose with, often inventing a new notation for each new piece of work. In the years leading up to the formation of the Scratch Orchestra, Cardew had produced a massive 200 page graphical score called *Treatise* which was his own attempt to exhaustively explore the creation of a musical practice that would 'encourage improvisation'**4** through a new graphical language. In today's terms, we might say that the

Survival Scrapbooks

Scratch-books were a way of turning the *Treatise* project over to a form of 'open source' development. The Scratch Orchestra employed a loose collaborative process of many individuals working in their own way towards a shared end. The analogy does not follow through entirely, Scratch-books were, on the whole, not exchanged between members, and there was little sense of incremental development or peer-review that exists in software development. As a form of authorship, however, certain parallels can be found: there was a conscious decision to keep Scratch-books unrestricted by copyright, and each score was seen as a possible accompaniment to another person's performance as well as a potential solo in its own right. This latter aspect can be compared to a common feature of Free and Open Source Software in that projects are frequently built as libraries that can be used as components in other projects ('accompaniments') as well as self-contained tools in their own right ('solos').

The contents of Scratch-books were hugely varied including adaptations of conventional music notation, abstract geometric shapes, flow diagrams, doodles, written instructions, and newspaper cuttings.[5] Although individuals were free to create scores in any manner they chose, the Scratch Orchestra's constitution, written by Cardew, defined how the production of Scratch-books fitted into the general practice of the Orchestra - members, for example, were advised to write no more than one piece per day.[6] This is one indicator of the internal conflicts and contradictions in the Scratch Orchestra which led to its break up in 1971. Although the Scratch Orchestra was loosely defined as an open platform, and a high degree of consensual autonomy between members was encouraged, there are many signs that Cardew looked upon it, perhaps unconsciously, as his own 'composition'. This is evident in aspects of the constitution and also in Cardew's own later criticisms of the Orchestra, in which he saw the spontaneous actions of some members, particularly a sub-group known as the Slippery Merchants of which Szczelkun was a part, as undermining the Scratch Orchestra project as a whole.[7] The demise of the Orchestra came when Cardew, under the encouragement of John Tilbury and Keith Rowe, began to apply Maoist ideological principles to the running of the group, which to many seemed like an attempt to assert authority over it thus leading to a split.[8]

The conflicts in the Scratch Orchestra are possibly presaged in Cardew's working notes to *Treatise*. In these he struggles with the potential contradictions of

> **Access to Tools is clearly a British version of the Whole Earth Catalogue**

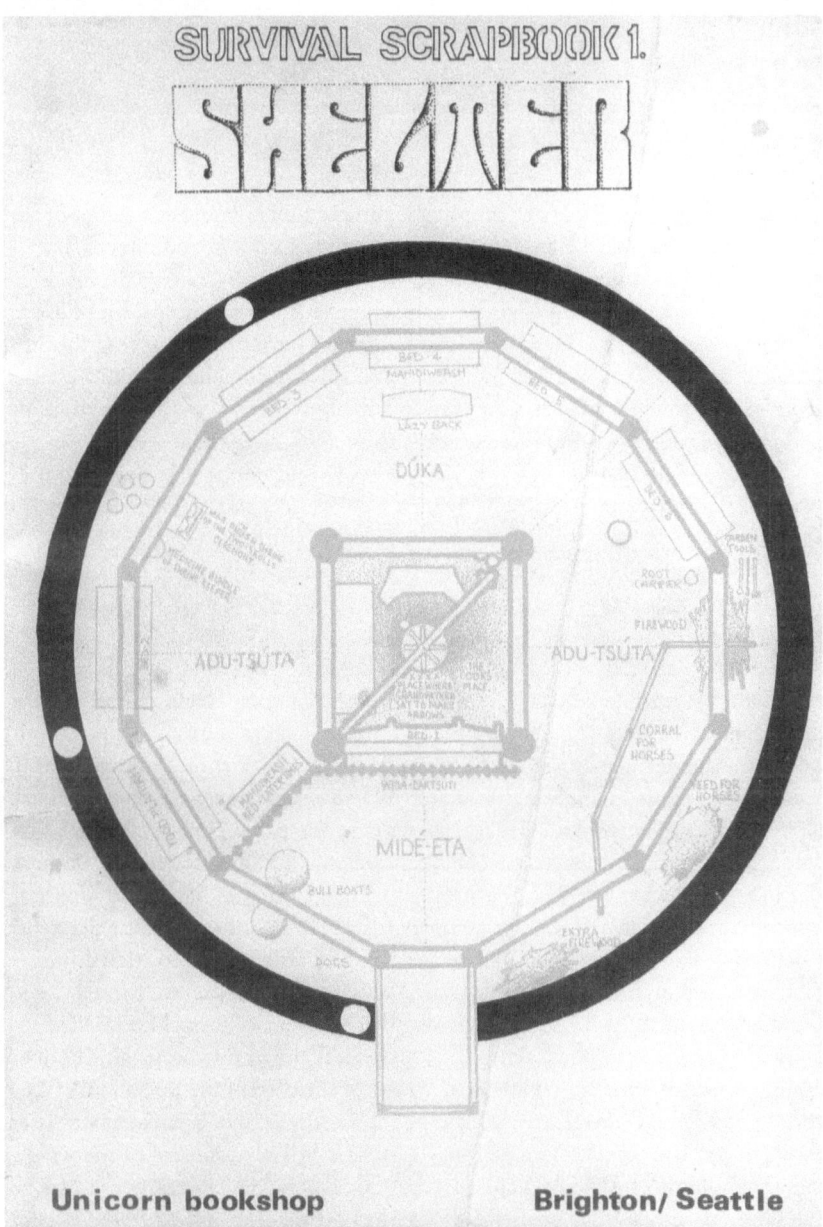

creating a definitive document, a music score, for an open-ended form of practice, improvisation. Cardew's desire to encourage improvisation is haunted by a fear of the arbitrary:

> The score must govern the music. It must have authority, and not merely be an arbitrary jumping-off point for improvisation, with no internal consistency.[9]

Image: Cover of *Survival Scrapbook Volume 1: Shelter*

The issue of governance is not simply one of how things sound but rather of how people behave. For Cardew, notations do not describe sound directly, but rather suggest possible practices through which sounds may emerge. In his references to Wittgenstein, 'to imagine a language means to imagine a form of life', Cardew's reflections on *Treatise* and improvisation move towards seeing this in terms of social praxis. The transition from the solitary composer working on a score to an ensemble collectively generating many scores follows from this, as do, perhaps, the problems of governance that arose along with that.

As information structures, the Scratch-books and Scrapbooks come from two quite different traditions. The Scratch-books are explorations in response to issues of notation, the abstract, formalised encoding of practices of production, whilst the Scrapbooks can be related to the chapbook as described by Szczelkun in his later analyses of the Exploding Cinema booklets.[10] Chapbooks were a form of mass publication that were popular in the 18th Century. They combined a variety of textual styles and content including histories, songs, and disparate types of artwork. Chapbooks were a part of both the popular and radical culture of their day, and are comparable to modern forms such as the fanzine. Notation and the chapbook can be related to James A. Scott's distinction between *techne* and *metis* as forms of knowledge practice.[11] He defines *techne* as a practice based around formal, abstract knowledge, and *metis* as one based around informal, situated, rule-of-thumb knowledge. The Scratch-books could be seen as an attempt to utilise *metis* in service of *techne*, whilst the Scrapbooks, in many ways do the opposite, appropriating *techne* in support of *metis*. Put another way, the Scratch Orchestra could be seen, from the perspective of Cardew's compositional interests, as an exploration of how to turn improvisational practice into formal knowledge, whilst the Scrapbooks seek to make aspects of formal knowledge available to improvisational practice. In both cases the improvisational is both an aesthetic and an ethic, social and artistic, but in the case of the Scrapbooks, the social potential is more clearly worked out and addressed, as Szczelkun was later to write: 'aesthetics follows an integrity of action.'[12] The aesthetics of the scrapbooks is not one of conventional artistic product, however, but one of survival, the sensuous appraisal of existence. It may be that the problems with the Scratch Orchestra, as Cardew saw them, came from an inability to match the contingencies of individual actions against the desired aesthetic integrity of notation and music as a communicative whole. In the Scrapbooks, the integrity of action arises, perhaps paradoxically, from the very un-integrated nature of the scrapbook format, one destined to fall apart and re-assemble in new unplanned-for structures. For the integrity of action in the Scrapbooks is the integrity of the distributive principle that underlines them:

This is a guide to what is possible. The way to learn about these things is to do them. The way to change is through open action; so get out and do it, and let people know about it.[13]

Footnotes

[1] For Szczelkun's own analysis of his involvement in these different groups see his *Art Collectives: Exploding Cinema 1992 - 1999, culture and democracy*, PhD thesis, 2002, available online at: http://www.stefan-szczelkun.org.uk/.

[2] See Wikipedia entry on Friedrich Wilhelm August Fröbel, http://en.wikipedia.org/wiki/Froebel.

[3] Stefan Szczelkun, 1972, *Survival Scrapbook 1: Shelter*, Brighton: Unicorn Bookshop, inside front cover.

[4] Cornelius Cardew, 1974, *Stockhausen Serves Imperialism*, p.79, originally published by Latimer New Directions (London), available as an electronic document from http://www.ubu.com/historical/cardew/cardew.html.

[5] A collection of examples from Scratch-books were published by Latimer New Directions in 1972, and later reprinted as: Cornelius Cardew, et al., 1974, *Scratch Music*, Cambridge, MA: MIT Press.

[6] The constitution is reproduced in the *Scratch Music* book.

[7] For different views on the history and break up of the Scratch Orchestra see Cardew's self-criticism in *Stockhausen Serves Imperialism*, Szczelkun's account in 'Art Collectives' (http://www.stefan-szczelkun.org.uk/phd102.htm, and http://www.stefan-szczelkun.org.uk/PHD-SCRATCH2.html), John Tilbury's article on Cardew for the *Journal of Experimental Music Studies* (http://www.users.waitrose.com/%7echobbs/tilburycardew.html), and the films *Journey to the North Pole: Cornelius Cardew and the Scratch Orchestra*, 1971, by Hanne Boenisch, and *Pilgrimage From Scattered Points*, 2006, by Luke Fowler.

[8] The break up of the Orchestra may also have been symptomatic of many of the problems that those experimenting with non-hierarchical collectives in this time experienced, such as discussed in Jo Freeman's "The Tyranny of Structurelessness", 1972, available online at: http://www.jofreeman.com/joreen/tyranny.htm.

[9] Cornelius Cardew, 1971, *Treatise Handbook*, London: Edition Peters, p. iv.

[10] Part of 'Art Collectives', http://www.stefan-szczelkun.org.uk/phd701.htm.

[11] James C. Scott, 1998, *Seeing Like a State: How Certain Schemes to Improve the Human Condition Have Failed*, New Haven and London: Yale University Press.

[12] Stefan Szczelkun, 1990, 'Artists' Liberation', in *Class Myths and Culture*, London: Working Press, p. 28.

[13] Stefan Szczelkun, 1972, *Survival Scrapbook 2: Food*, Brighton: Unicorn Bookshop, inside front cover.

Simon Yuill is an artist and programmer based in Glasgow, Scotland. He is a developer in the *spring_alpha* and Social Versioning System (SVS) projects. He has helped setup and run a number of hacklab and free media labs in Scotland including the Chateau Institute of Technology (ChIT) and Electron Club, as well as the Glasgow branch of OpenLab. He has written on aspects of Free Software and cultural praxis and has contributed to publications such as Software Studies (MIT Press, 2008), the FLOSS Manuals and Digital Artists Handbook project (GOTO10 and Folly)

Now that environmentalists and government ostensibly have the same interests at heart one might expect a bit of collusion. But the Climate Camp at London's Heathrow Airport last month saw protesters, media and the police co-produce an event of extraordinary restraint, reports <u>Damian Abbott</u>. While the Met made the protesters' lives as difficult as possible, the campers seemed to be doing a pretty good job of this on their own

CLIMATE CAMP 2007: ANOTHER END OF THE WORLD IS POSSIBLE

Tuesday 14 August: outside Staines BR station and it's raining. Pissing down, and despite being medically ill-disposed to tents, mud, and more fucking rain, I'm asking someone holding a leaflet that states 'You are not fucked' for directions to the camp site. He sends me, and a couple of others, over to a white hire van. The driver looks frazzled, he has apparently been on the go since seven in the morning, and drives us at a sedate pace along the dual carriageways that feed traffic towards the north of Heathrow airport. He's been stopped and searched several times, and responded, 'I don't know' to numerous questions, except for the necessary name and address. Understandably, he's feeling a bit singled out, but I don't think the

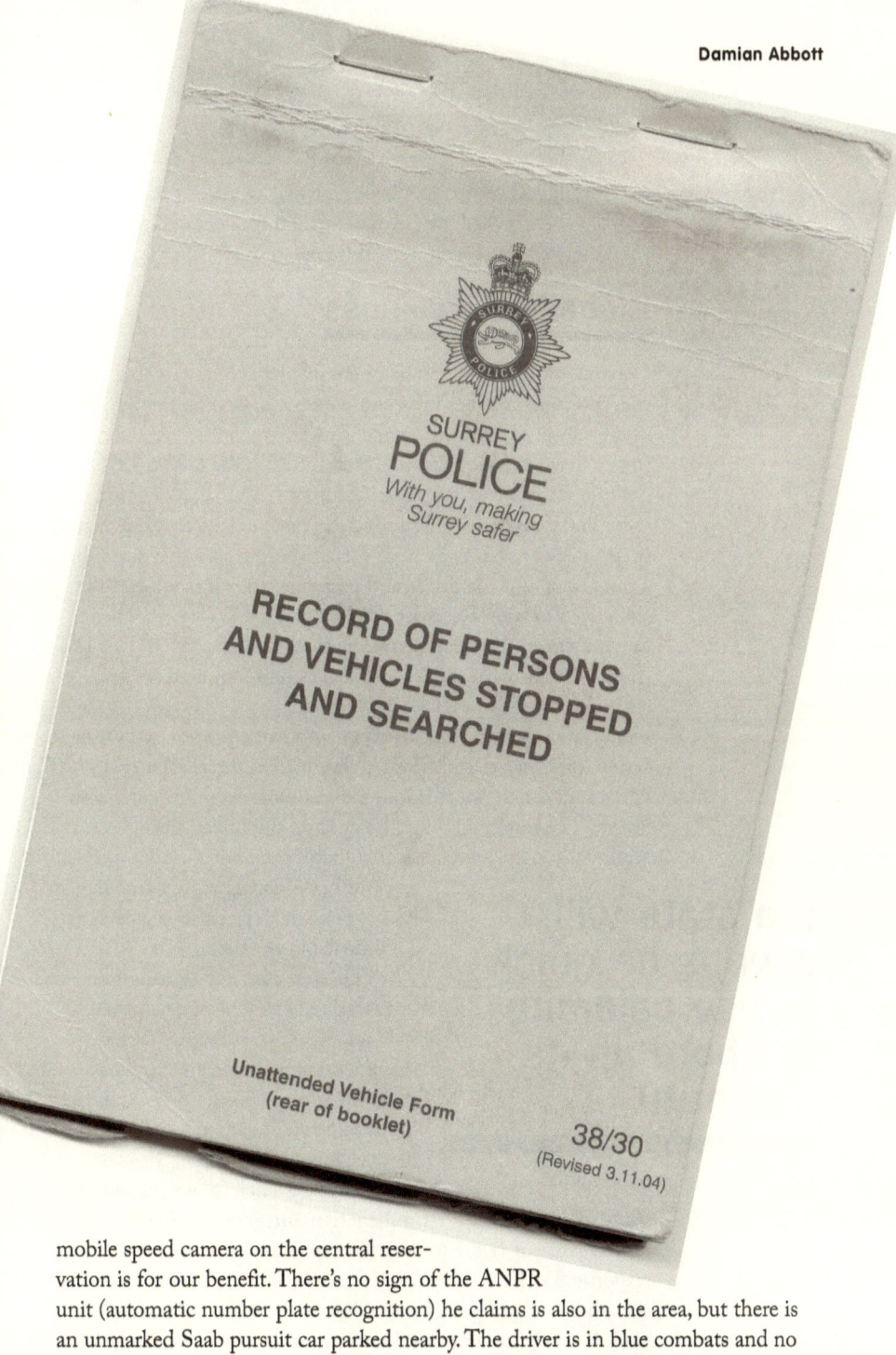

mobile speed camera on the central reservation is for our benefit. There's no sign of the ANPR unit (automatic number plate recognition) he claims is also in the area, but there is an unmarked Saab pursuit car parked nearby. The driver is in blue combats and no fluorescent vest, so not your average traffic grunt, but the only people getting pulled over fit the usual profile: young black men, young white men, young men. Business as usual.

Globalised Business

Gatsometer, a Dutch company, are involved in researching image encryption techniques (as a consequence of developing the use of digital speed cameras), while Truvelo [http://www.truvelouk.com/], established in the UK in 1993, describe themselves as a manufacturer of 'Traffic law enforcement and data gathering products'. Truvelo make handheld laser speed guns, as well as forward facing speed cameras (that enable a photograph of the driver and passenger to be taken), and the 'Moving Violation Recorder with Digital EyeWitness®.' Their South African sister company, Truvelo Manufacturers (PTY) Ltd [http://www.truvelo.co.za/], also makes high-powered sniper rifles and an array of carbines. Both companies are in the avant-garde of establishing the mechanisms of an automated process, producing a system of justice that removes an event from the particularities of its causation, and places it into the irrational realm of moral absolutism. The threshold that differentiates the citizen from the criminal is so precisely measured that it becomes a border without any width, the consequence being that it is only possible to be either a citizen or a criminal, but not both.

> **the state will always be quick to use calamity to shore up its authority**

This side-effect of globalisation, an increased tendency towards an extensive, totalising, and absolute system of reference, seems to me also to produce the more millenarian tendencies of the social movement gathering around climate change issues. While the state will always be quick to use calamity to shore up its authority, its 'millenarian' antagonists oppose a simplified sense of virtue to both the perceived crisis and the state's response. Far from offering an analysis of globalisation, they remain its offspring, its inevitable waste product. For instance, *Only Planet* (the camp handbook given to all arrivals by the 'welcome team') states clearly that any change in the climate does not affect us all equally and makes a statistical argument that air travel is a class issue, citing an average salary of £48,000 for passengers from British airports. Absent, though, is any discussion about the nature of working-class transnational mobility. Absent too is any sign of awareness as to how the demand to 'be more realistic about whether the entire human race can afford for you to go on your holidays' [sic] (*Only Planet* again) plays into the hands of right-wingers, who would readily use the impending doom scenario to curb immigration. Telling people to stay at home, assumes that they have a 'home' in the first place, indeed it assumes a degree of comfort with the very idea of a national identity. 'Social change, not lifestyle change', is the demand on one prominent banner that I see later in the day, secured to a marquee in the centre of the site, but the obscurantist belief, the ersatz nationalism, that seems to be required has more in common with a faith than with any revolution that I can readily identify with.

Hydraulic Pressure

The road leading up to the camp has been closed to traffic, so we get out of the van. I'm interested in knowing which Act has been used to block off a public road, but the grunt on duty will only offer the somewhat occult answer of 'Commissioner's directions'. It's not until I walk further down the road that it's evident to what degree the camp is being scrutinised. A towering hydraulic arm suspends CCTV cameras in the air, and police floodlights enhance the notion of the camp as being an arena, as well as acting as a light source of psychological pressure. When the Tour de France cut its way through London this summer, the effect was no less intense, and all the accoutrements of contemporary sporting spectacle are here, right down to the journalists tapping towards an evening deadline on wireless equipped laptops, in cars parked on the camp's periphery. Any casual passer-by might come up with the same analogy, since the land being squatted by the Climate Camp is part of Harlington Sports Ground. This may have been an astute choice of trespass: the sports fields are owned by Imperial College and are currently under threat of a Compulsory Purchase Order to facilitate Heathrow's expansion. Since CPOs rarely match a property's potential market value, I'm sure Imperial College will already have approached BAA with some tentative negotiations, offering to speed the sale for the right deal. Equally, it's likely, though not by any means sure, that an academic institution would move slowly to force an eviction: one eye on maintaining an image of civility; another eye on sections of the student body that might be supportive of the camp's aims. A prolonged or high-level news 'incident' would threaten to bring disruption to the

Climate Camp 2007

campus when everyone returns after the summer, and might also raise awkward questions as to whether the land was originally acquired with knowledge of its potential value to the operators of Heathrow. For their part, the squatters managed the camp's representation to local residents (up to 2000 of whom face eviction and are running their own campaign: http://www.notrag.org), as carefully as they managed its media representation, letters describing the camp's aims being sent to most households in the vicinity.

Ninjas of Data Collection

A Forward Intelligence Team (FIT) is busy doing its thing at the camp entrance. If the camp seeks to authenticate its authority with an image of virtue, then Forward Intelligence policing is its antithesis. Forward Intelligence is primarily about intimidation, and has been adopted even at the most quotidian levels of maintaining public order. Their most visible incarnation is the FIT photographer. The blue baseball cap and combats are intended to give the impression that they are brothers-in-arms with their American cousins in S.W.A.T, or their cooler, Gallic comrades in the CRS. These ninjas of data

Image: Stop and search sheet found at Climate Camp

82 Mute - Climate for Change Special Edition

collection carry cameras with a huge lens, large flash, and an attached digital camera, so that it resembles some kind of bio-mechanical prosthesis. The uniform belies the fact that Britain is one of the few European countries not to have a barracked, paramilitary police force; FIT photographers are more like paparazzi that have lost any index of their subject's economic value and now take photos indiscriminately. Anyone is fair game, you merely have to come into the lens' field of view to merit a snap.

Such an indiscriminate collection of data can have little real intelligence value in the traditional sense. I'm sure we're meant to believe that they possess an arcane knowledge of 'hidden Markov chains' and 'dynamic link matching' that has spawned accurate facial recognition algorithms (ones that perform consistently across the genders, that don't get confused by expressions of emotion), powering a RapidResponse™ database. I have no doubt that this is their desired future, but for now, FIT policing relies on the fact that we actually care about being seen. I'm not sure if my photo is taken as I arrive, since the paparazzo are dithering between the choice of capturing an old gentleman on his bicycle or a couple stretching a banner between them on which is written 'Prevent Privacy Invasion', or some such legend. (I thought the point of squatting *was* to question the notion of privacy and private property in general, but at this point of the day I was actively trying not to be a source of schismatic, hair-splitting argument...). After my last brush with public order policing, enough DNA was collected to clone an army of me, so I'm not too bothered. If understood merely as intimidation then FIT is something of a short-term strategy. In a world where everyone carries a camera, we no longer believe that the lens steals our souls, but perhaps the FIT methods must be seen as an acknowledgement that traditional forms of intelligence gathering have limited value in the face of an increas-

> **right-wingers would readily use the impending doom scenario to curb immigration**

ingly heterogeneous 'threat'. It is the other state response to globalisation, another form of surrendering to the irrational, but in this case rather than seeking to homogenise instances of the particular, make them recognisable under a single scheme of identification, it seeks simply to revel in them. That the activity has some kind of formal use is the cover for an orgiastic indulgence, the side effects of which are as yet unknown to the state. It hankers after effect, any effect, because it knows, at some base level, that in such eroticism there is power.

Voluntary Restraint

Conversely, it's a mark of almost all the actions that the camp builds up to on the Saturday that they involve some form of voluntary restraint or self-immolation. Rather than indulgence, there is denial. People lock themselves on to fences and gates. Workshops throughout the preceding week, train people in the art of superglueing their hands onto any available symbolic surface, in order to await the police solvents that will free them. Even the ritual of marching on the headquarters of BAA seems to be no more than a case of presenting oneself for temporary encirclement by a cordon of police officers, and submitting oneself to the gaze of the media. It's less a case of misfortune, and more a direct consequence of the mental and physical asceticism of the camp that the banner which dominated later news photos claimed the movement's desire to 'Make Planes History'. How are we to leave behind all desire for flight? We cannot. It's nonsense. Let's make more planes, let's make our own aircraft, our own, more varied types of flight... Gliders, airships, ground effect vehicles, types of craft as yet untested and types of craft as yet unknown. Let's counter the state's indiscriminate gaze with the full extent of our own desires, the full extent of who we are. At the limits of prediction, it's tempting to revert to the foetal, but if the task is truly one of transformation then the tactics of restraint should not be allowed to control and dominate the heterogeneous outcomes of playful chaos.

I receive updates on the progress of the actions from Indymedia, via text messages:

Damian Abbott

20/08/07 08:03:35 IMCUK: Sizewell nuclear power station blockaded by five people in concrete lock-ons. Banner reads 'nuclear power is not the answer to climate chaos'.

20/08/07 11:21:01 IMCUK: Sizewell B blockade still in place. No cutting team present yet. All the media and all but one of the support team move down the road.

20/08/07 13:57:48 IMCUK: As recently as 1:30pm, Sizewell B blockade still in place after six hours and still no cutting team present.

20/08/07 14:04:18 IMCUK: Sizewell B blockaders have called in to report they packed up five minutes ago, walking off without arrest. Now on their way home, wet but happy.

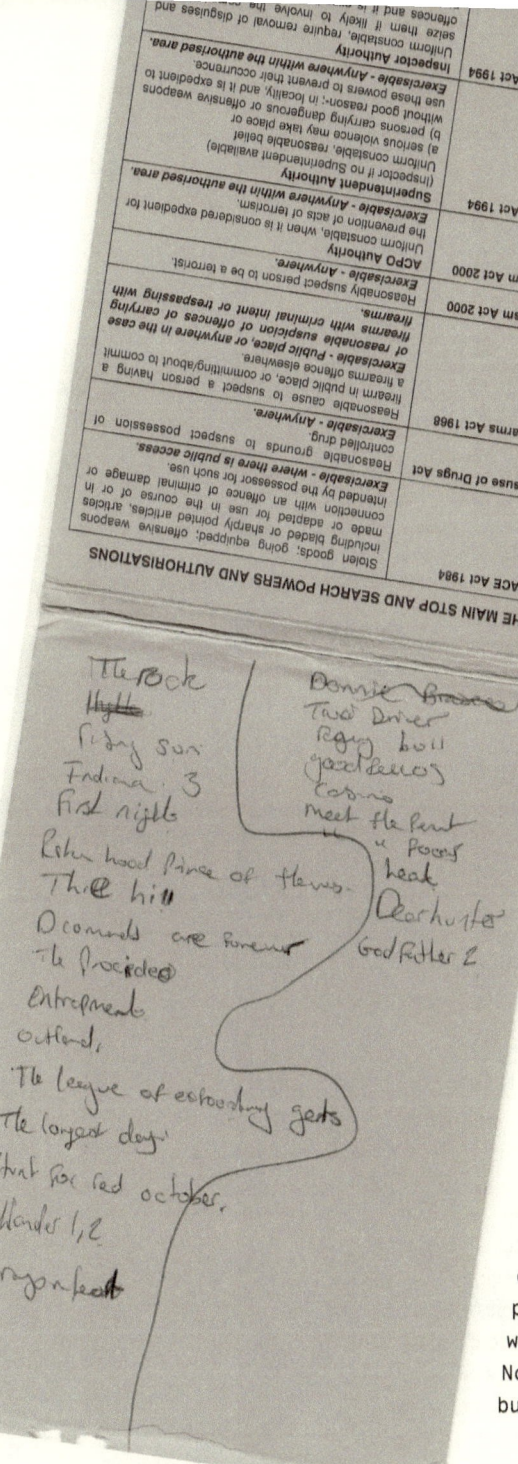

Image: Stop and search sheet found at Climate Camp

It's Not Easy Being Green

Climate Camp 2007

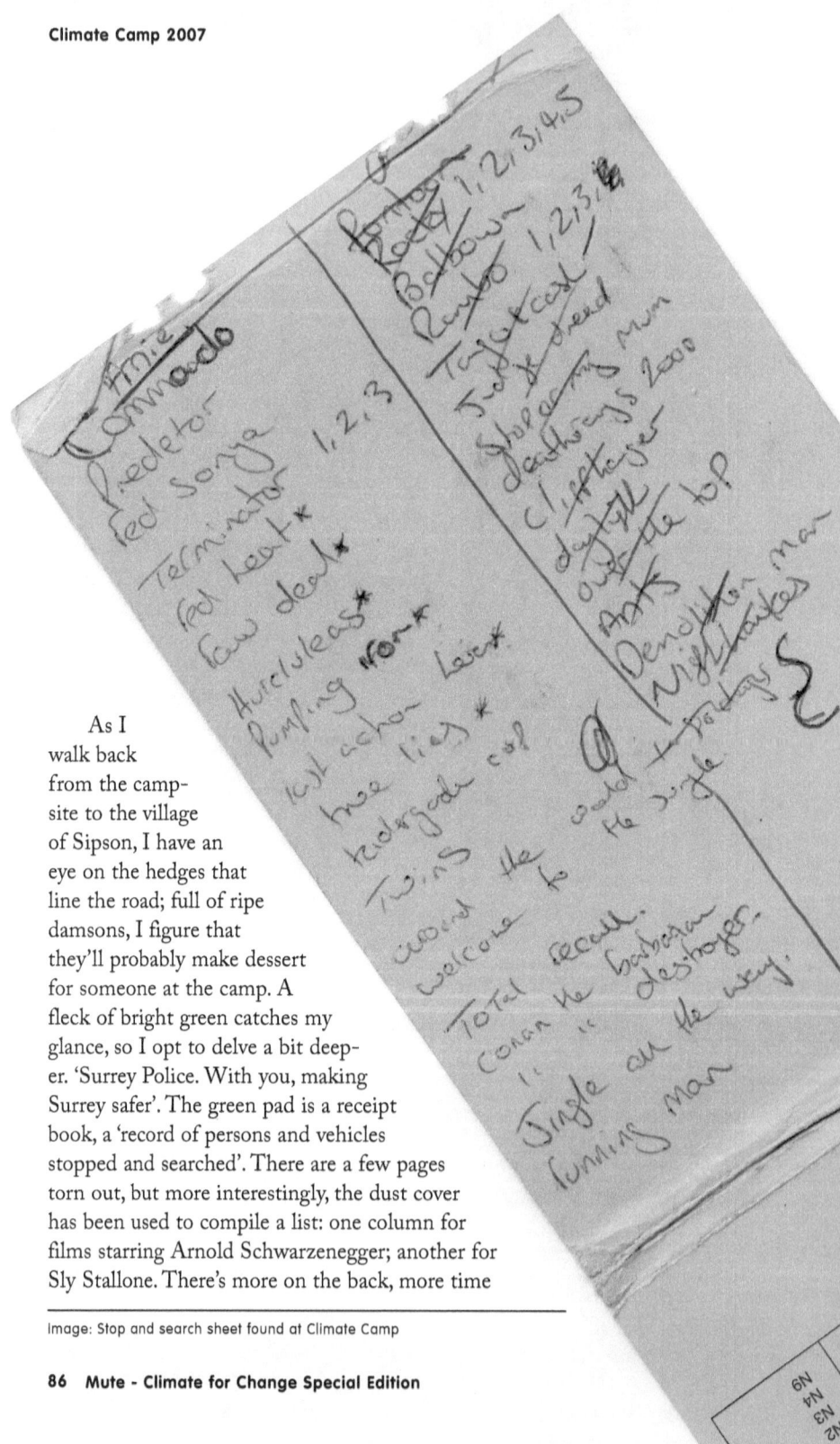

As I walk back from the campsite to the village of Sipson, I have an eye on the hedges that line the road; full of ripe damsons, I figure that they'll probably make dessert for someone at the camp. A fleck of bright green catches my glance, so I opt to delve a bit deeper. 'Surrey Police. With you, making Surrey safer'. The green pad is a receipt book, a 'record of persons and vehicles stopped and searched'. There are a few pages torn out, but more interestingly, the dust cover has been used to compile a list: one column for films starring Arnold Schwarzenegger; another for Sly Stallone. There's more on the back, more time

Image: Stop and search sheet found at Climate Camp

filled by a random process of indexing. I wonder how the pad came to be in the hedge and hope that it wasn't carelessly dropped, or conspiratorially placed. There's always the possibility that having completed this list it dawned on our constable that he had a few more lists of his own to complete. And none of them involved the random designation of old men on bicycles as 'terrorists'. But there's no empty and abandoned uniform to be found, not in this hedge at least. Perhaps someone decided being an object at the orgy was nowhere near as much fun as taking part, and decided to take back a little of that erotic power. Perhaps that person tried to put the little receipt book in a place where neither the sun nor floodlights shine. Futile as that gesture might be as an isolated, individualised instance, it's the mark of a particular kind of absence that I leave, hungry for a complex unmediated moment.

Info

The Climate Camp took place near Heathrow Airport, London, 14-21 August 2007

Damian Abbott <damian AT fiercesociology.org> is a co-founder and editor of *Inventory* and has worked under various pseudonyms on other collective enterprises

> From the 'greening of immigration controls' to diktats to eat less, work more, pay extra for energy and waste, there appears to be an increasing tendency for green politics to lean towards repressive measures as solutions to the environmental crisis. **Manchester No Borders** tackle the controversial idea of 'overpopulation'

'OVERPOPULATION': LETTING CAPITALISM OFF THE HOOK

From when we started being active as a No Borders group in Manchester we have been frustrated with a lack of radical analyses and critiques (anti-state, anti-authoritarian, anti-capitalist, anti-discrimination etc.) of climate change. This was particularly so, as we became aware of a 'greening of immigration controls'. There appears to be an increasing tendency for green politics to lean towards repressive measures as solutions to the environmental crisis.

More specifically, in discussions with other (environmental) activists, we have recently found ourselves in disagreement over the issue of 'overpopulation'. A common green orthodoxy today is that there are too many people on this planet, and that we need to do something about it. (Although we gave a well-attended workshop at the Climate Camp on this topic and we were positively surprised how many of the participants were critical of this stance.)

In this article, we want to spell out the dangers of the 'the planet is full' argument and argue that 'overpopulation' is not the root cause of climate change. Not people are the problem, but society. Not human beings *per se*, but the way our social life is organized: capitalism.

There are two levels to our criticism of the 'overpopulation' argument. One, the argument quite simply plays into the hands of governments, nationalists and anti-feminists who are quite happy to step up demographic controls, people management and anti-immigration policies. Two, interpreting population growth as the root cause of the climate crisis completely disregards the systemic nature of the problem and thus lets capitalism off the hook.

The Overpopulation Argument

So where is the problem? The UN projects that world population figures will rise from today's 6.8 billion to 9.2 billion by 2050. For the prophets of demographic doom, Britain, in particular, is under threat. Government projections are that the UK population is to rise from 60.6 million (mid-2006) to 77 million in 2050. Obviously, demographic modelling contains lots of cultural and political assumptions, and should be treated as politically informed rather than neutral observations. Human population behaviour is very random and unpredictable and not something that can be forecasted as unproblematically as tomorrow's weather, say (and you know how inaccurate that is!).

> A common green orthodoxy today is that there are too many people on this planet

Whatever the assumption, an increasing amount of global players (from government agencies to international organizations, from think tanks to celebrities) conclude that the planet is full. They argue that any such densely populated area as Britain would be unsustainable in terms of food production, housing and energy needs. Also within the green movement this is not a marginal position and no longer limited to 'deep ecologists'. The green-nationalist think tank 'Optimum Population Trust', for example, estimates that the UK can only sustain less than half its current population level. And they demand a national population policy that first stabilizes the number of people in the UK and then gradually brings it down to 30 million.

The fact is however, that the UK population is growing primarily because of immigration. The argument thus is threefold.

'Overpopulation': Letting Capitalism off the Hook

First, immigration puts pressure on national resources such as water, energy, food and countryside. Second, new migrants tend to have more children than the national population thereby accelerating the problem. Third, migration to 'first world' countries turns previously low-impact consumers into high-impact consumers increasing their ecological footprints. It comes as no surprise to us, then, that the BNP calls itself the 'real Green Party'.

The government's chief green advisor, Jonathan Porritt, has also time and again argued this point. But what to do? Porritt's suggestion is straightforward: zero net immigration! David Cameron also agrees that rapid population increase will put pressure on our natural resources. And again, his solution is to lower net immigration:

> my focus today is on population, and here we should note that only around thirty per cent of the projected increase in our population by 2031 is due to higher birth rates and longer life-spans…the evidence shows that roughly seventy per cent - more than two thirds - of the increase in our population each year is attributable to net migration. Of that increase, forty seven per cent comes directly from people moving to Britain, and the rest from higher birth rates amongst immigrant populations.

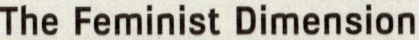

Manchester No Borders

The Feminist Dimension

It becomes clear that in a sexist, imperialist, capitalist world, it is impossible to separate discussion of population control from hierarchies of oppression. Which population is going to be "controlled" and how will this control come about?

Any form of population control risks seriously impinging upon women's right to bodily autonomy. State-enforced population control programs, such as China's 'one-child policy', are usually enacted upon women's bodies; it is women who are forced to have abortions, to undergo sterilisation, or to take long-term birth control products (often with serious health repercussions). Rarely are men forced to undergo vasectomies, despite the relative easiness of this procedure when compared to tubal ligation.

However, not all women will be affected equally; those from the Global South, ethnic minorities, those perceived as disabled, and the working class have historically borne the brunt of population control policies. Eugenicists in Victorian England were very clear about which segments of the population needed controlling: the poor and the disabled.

More recently, Black British feminists in the 1970s and 1980s wrote about the need to campaign for abortion rights while at the same time also fighting for their right *not* to have abortions and *not* to be pressured into sterilisation. At the same time dangerous forms of birth control, like early experimental forms of Depo-Provera, were being tested upon women in the Global South (and in predominantly African-American areas of the US) before being allowed for sale in the Western world. Today, women in the Global South are often 'encouraged' by NGOs to use long-term forms of birth control, like implants, that require medical attention to stop (as opposed to something like The Pill, which can be stopped at any time by the woman taking it). This history cannot be ignored today when discussing population control in the UK. As single working-class mothers, immigrants and ethnic minorities (particularly Muslims) find themselves being increasingly demonised; any population control policies will target women from these groups.

Malthus

Throughout its history then the overpopulation argument has been used to present people and children as the source of inherently social problems: letting capitalism off the hook. The argument always goes like this: there are too many of us and the planet can't hack it. Whether it's the poor, the Jews, women or migrants, all have been used strategically as scapegoats for an irrational and unproductive use of space and resources within a capitalist economy.

One of the most prominent writers on over-population was Thomas Malthus, a 19th century cleric of the Church of England. His treatise on over-population *A summary view of the principle of population* was printed in 1830, but is still read widely today. Malthus stated that whilst population increased at a geometric rate (1, 2, 4, 8, 16…), doubling every 25 years, food production increases at an arithmetic rate (1, 2, 3, 4, 5…). Malthus believed this disparity between food production and population growth was the root cause of 'checks to (human) growth' such as war, famine and disease.

The strong strand of prejudice within Malthus' work, however, often goes unacknowledged by neo-Malthusianists. He saw poverty as deserved rather than produced and blamed the poor for their 'lack of moral restraint' thus making them the primary focus of population policy. The inherent conservatism and class prejudice hidden behind a veneer of scientific objectivity has made Malthus a popular source of intellectual legitimacy for various conservative and authoritarian positions.

In the late 19th century eugenicists began utilising and expanding on Malthus's critique of the rapid population growth of the poor. Eugenicists argued that this lack of restraint was genetically inherited and posed a threat to the future of the nation. A prominent eugenicist was Winston Churchill and many discriminatory laws were passed to attempt to influence the outcome of breeding. Once again

> **Porritt's suggestion is straightforward: zero net immigration!**

systemic problems were naturalised and projected upon the very people most negatively affected by them.

Neo-Malthusianism

Many anti-migration authors have also mobilised Malthusian ideas. These arguments have relied upon an analysis of national resources as closed and finite systems and exaggerating rates of migration. Proposals for the closing of borders are contrasted with images of swarms of migrants exhausting national resources like locust. One example of this nationalist position, which supports the competitive nature of states, is this quote from the *Population and environment* journal:

> Countries that are in the lead in reducing their populations should not give in to advocates of growth by allowing massive immigration. This rewards those who multiply irresponsibly

As environments change due to climate change the monster of 'overpopulation' is being resurrected as a security issue. As we are seeing with climate change, environmental issues provide a space for the legitimisation of conservative and authoritarian policies.

Perhaps one of the most influential of these authors was Garrett Hardin whose essay 'The Tragedy of the Commons', printed in 1968, masked a pro-private property stance beneath a veneer of scientific objectivity. Hardin believed that, without private ownership of natural resources, unchecked population growth would lead to their exhaustion. The same arguments were used to support the 20th century 'green revolution' and are appearing again with the G8 leaders in Japan agreeing to extend research into GM crops to deal with 'overpopulation'. 'Overpopulation' is used as a convenient argument to support the agendas of specific political and economic actors.

But let's not attack a straw man here. None of the green progressives here in the UK argue for more stringent migration controls (in contrast to parts of the green conservationist movement in the US). Nonetheless, we have witnessed population graphs being used in climate change presentations, which could have lead to knee-jerk reactions and dangerous political conclusions when taken out their left-wing context.

Earth First?

The climate action movement of course recognises the repression faced by migrants and the fact that the groups of people who are hit hardest by climate change are in the Global South. However, even with the best intentions of warding off ecological destruction and creating better lives for people in the face of climate chaos the 'overpopulation' argument still ignores the systemic logic behind climate change: capitalism.

The central flaw to Malthusian thought is its a-systemic nature. Regardless of the economic system or social organisation, it views the root cause of most human suffering as population growth, and in particular the threat of the poor becoming richer (and thus consuming more). Poverty, however, is produced not bred, and by projecting systemic flaws onto those it most affects neo-Malthusianism both helps to protect the status quo from criticism and construct vulnerable social groups as legitimate targets of control.

As relatively rich Western countries consume the most energy, it is often argued that it is their populations, in particular, that should be curbed, whether by authoritarian state control, or by individuals in the West simply realizing it is their moral responsibility not to reproduce. But to imply that the Earth should come before a child can lead down a dangerous path. It may lead to a resentment of those social groups that migrate or reproduce more often than others.

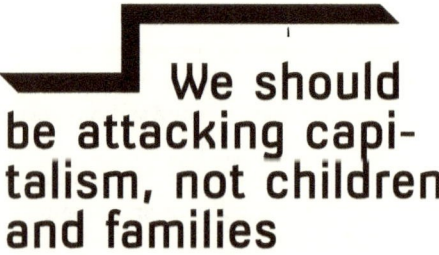
We should be attacking capitalism, not children and families

Besides, social, economic and cultural pressures to have or not to have children cannot be tackled through individual lifestyle choices and guilt trips. An emancipatory response to climate change requires a political and social solution.

We should be attacking capitalism, not children and families. In a world where children are killed over oil and exploited at the hands of multi-national corporations it isn't surprising that children will eventually be blamed for capitalism's fuck-ups. Capitalism doesn't make sense and neither do capitalist solutions. The 'overpopulation' argument ignores the contradictions inherent in capitalism that mediate the relationship between human beings and the environment and already limit our freedom and desires on a real everyday level.

Instead of acknowledging the unprecedented global disasters that seem to spiral as capitalism grows and spreads its destructive wings, the 'overpopulation' argument asks not for a new form of social organisation (that might see land and resources accessed and shared more evenly, contributing to less poverty, more sustainable lifestyles and fewer wars) but takes the shameful and hopeless route of asking people to have fewer children. In a world where we are repeatedly screwed over we are now being asked not to screw!

Notes
This article was originally published in *Shift* #4, September 2008.
www.shiftmag.co.uk

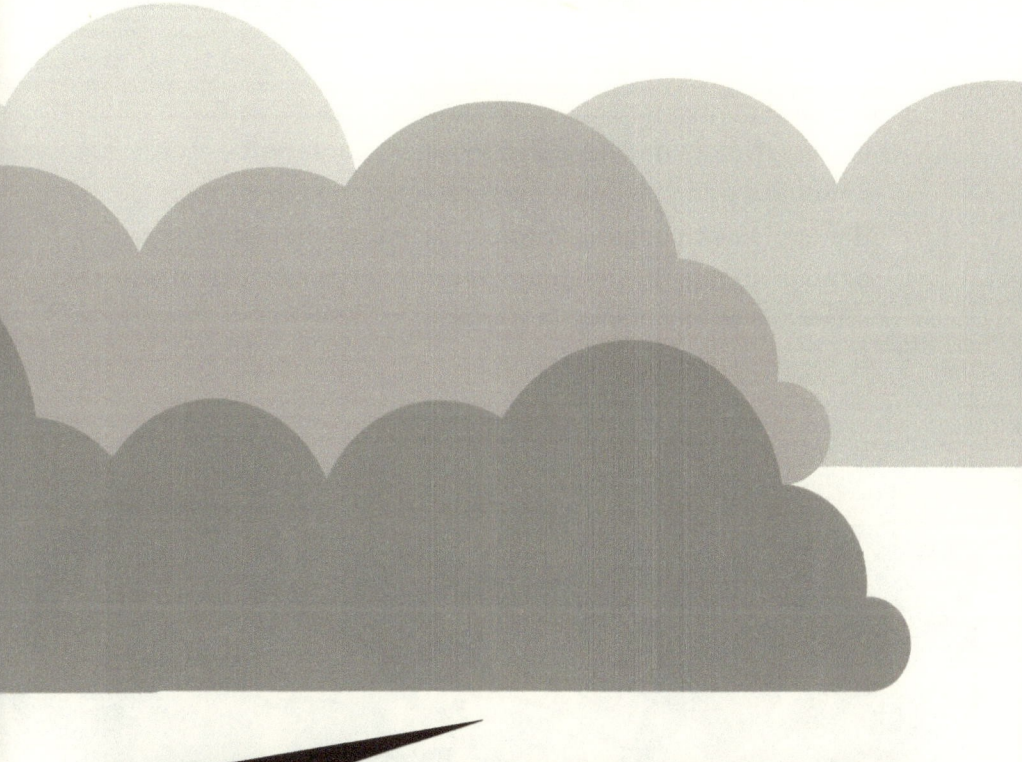

Manchester No Borders is a group 'resisting migration controls and the persecution, detention and exploitation of refugees and other migrants. We are committed to practical solidarity and direct action as well as imagining a world without borders and ways to realise this.' Recently, we have aimed to focus strongly on the theory linking border control, capitalism and the environment to help inform our practical actions resisting migration controls. This article is a product of these many discussions.
www.manchesternoborders.org.uk

A CLIMATIC DISORDER? CLASS, COAL AND CLIMATE CHANGE

At last November's NUM convened conference, trade unionists and Climate Campers were invited to debate the explosive cocktail of (clean) coal, class and climate change. John Cunningham reports on the frustrating attempts to find a middle ground

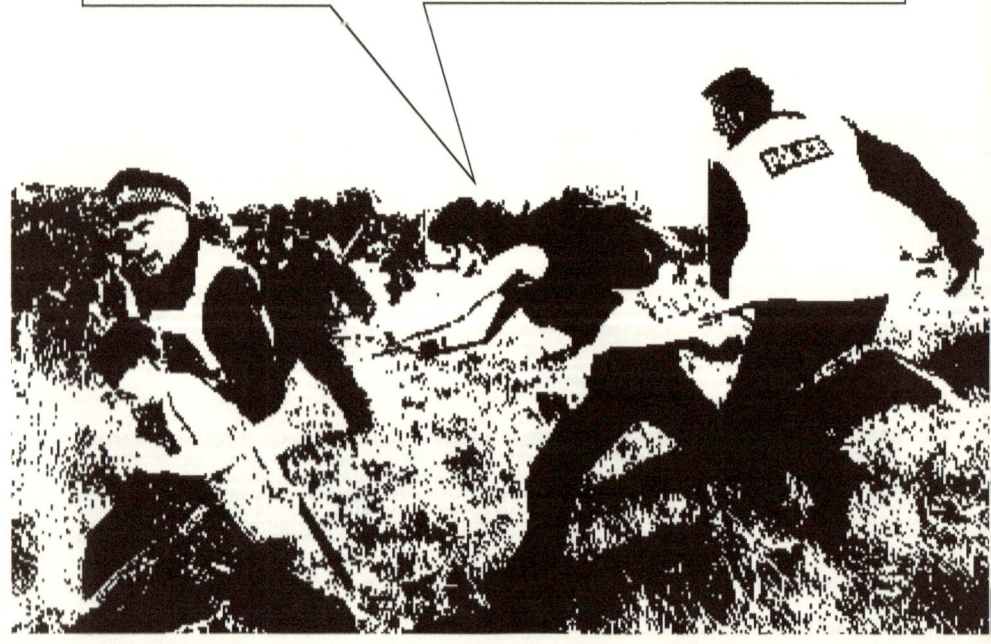

John Cunningham

This year's camp at Kingsnorth in Kent against the opening of a new coal fired power station produced a range of predictable responses, from the inanity of the *Guardian*'s suggestion that it was yet another alternative lifestyle festival, to the over zealous attentions of the security state. One of the more interesting responses was from long standing anarchist activist and ex-National Union of Mineworkers (NUM) official Dave Douglass. In a polemic against the camp, he addressed the anti-coal bias of the Climate Campers alongside a perceived lack of class analysis within the camp and the wider green movement. There is undoubtedly a feel good anti-capitalism implicit in much of the discourse around climate camp that can exclude any consideration of class in favour of blandly utopian sentiment. For instance, in the *Climate Camp Newspaper* statements such as 'Sometimes it feels as though our world is coloured in sadness. And you just want to be somewhere else…'[1] read less like a detournement of advertising copy than a self help approach to political activism, the 'middle class voice' that Douglass characteristically claimed Climate Camp spoke in.

At the time I was relieved that, against the fluffy anti-capitalism of much of the camp's official discourse, Douglass introduced the perspective of those who may not have 'somewhere else' to go, locked into jobs and communities that a politics of exodus cannot easily address. The yearly anti-climate change road-show attempts to offer a response to climate change that would destabilise business as usual, suggesting at least nominally anti-capitalist alternatives. However, its model of protest camp and sustainable community gleaned from the post-Seattle summit protests can seem too abstracted from everyday life to break the general perception that climate change exists 'out there', to be dealt with by super-heroes such as Al Gore. Its model of sustainability can also appear as a holiday in scarcity to the casual observer. The intervention by Douglass was a dose of messy actuality. The camp's response was to invite Douglass to address it, and he turned up with ex-NUM president, 'Old King Coal' himself, Arthur Scargill in tow. The Newcastle based conference, Class, Climate Change and Clean Coal – the Climate Campers and the Unions, sponsored by the NUM, the RMT and the Industrial Workers of the World (IWW), arose out of this dialogue.

> This is a sad and confusing conjuncture of forces.
> – Dave Douglass[2]

At least the intersection of labour and environmentalism in the Douglass/ NUM/ Climate Camp exchange punctured a certain spectacle of climate change: the accumulation of catastrophic images, millennial eco-fear and eco-friendly consumerism that can induce occasional dread and the desire to assume the crash position. The

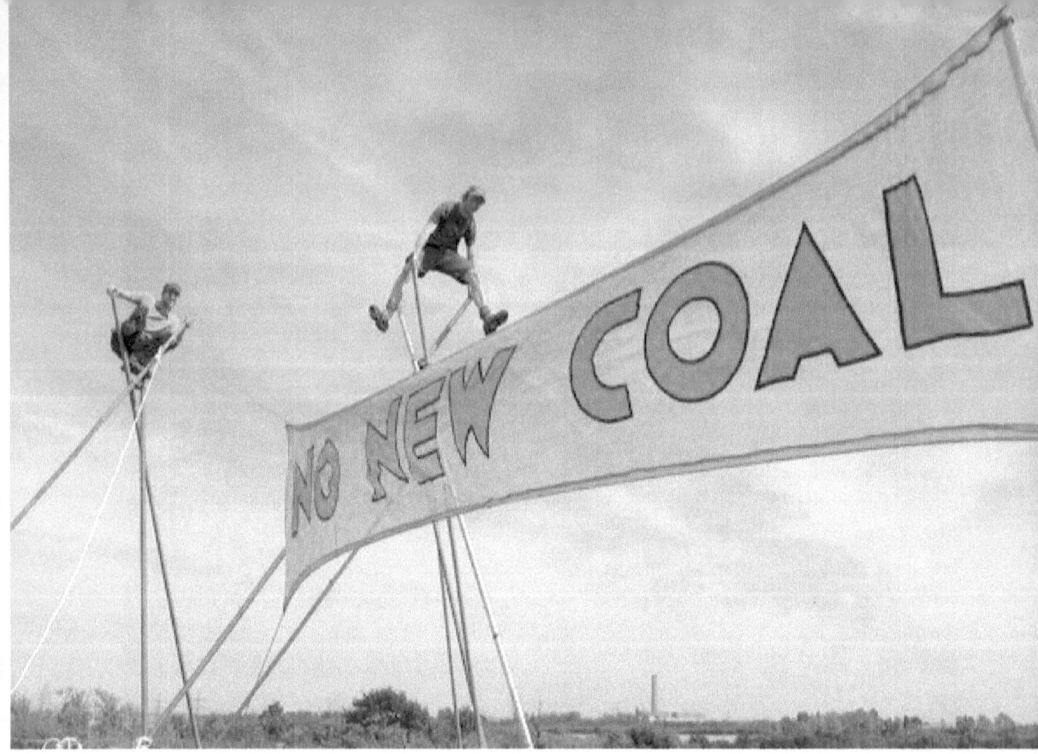

class tensions around Climate Camp seemed like a clash of cultures between a traditional 'mass worker' form of trade unionism and a diffuse network of activists whose politics ranged from pale green reformism to red and black anti-capitalism. In fairness to Climate Camp, they ran workshops on class and emphasised a 'just transition' in the official booklet's dialogue with workers in carbon-based industries. This is the notion that a transition can be made to a non-carbon based economy that does not penalise the poor or workers in carbon based industries such as coal miners. It is an argument for responses to climate change that place social justice at the forefront of any structural shift in the economy. While it is often posited as a decentralised, autonomous response, it can also be part of a social democratic state-led one, as Paul Chatterton's argument later in the conference for a 'green new deal' was to make clear.

While Douglass' intervention was welcome it also threatened to reduce a complex series of questions around class and climate change to the singular question of 'more prole than thou'. There's an admirable tenacity to the perpetuation of proletarian culture in the face of defeat and expropriation: many of the current pit banners at the miners' Durham Big Meeting gala are from defunct pits, less postmodern nostalgia than an assertion of community. However, this can harden into a closed identity as can the activist milieu around Climate Camp, with its own cultural and discursive forms and marginal counter-cultures that mean little to those outside.

I hoped that the conference would reveal something in common beyond a

Image: Tripods with Kingsnorth power station in the background, Climate Camp, Kent, 9 August 2008 shared preference for renewable energy and being anti-nuclear, points all the delegates made. The main point of contention in terms of energy policy was clean coal, based on carbon dioxide capture and storage, but the conjunction of more anti-capitalist elements from Climate Camp with the representatives of old school trade unionism also suggested other fault lines both cultural and political.[3]

Following the great tradition of working class radicals, the meeting was held in the Bridge Hotel pub in Newcastle, close to the industrial grandeur of the Tyne bridge and adjacent to the contemporary bubble of regeneration, cultural capital and service driven consumerism that is Newcastle today. A combination of NUM veterans, miners, trade unionists, eco-punks, socialists and maybe even one or two members of the general public attended the meeting. The conference delegates – NUM spokesmen, Climate Campers and a lone RMT spokesman – occupied a low wooden podium. Seated three at a time behind a desk, they sometimes gave the impression of a quarrelsome Stalinist tribunal. After a brief introduction by Keith Whittaker of the NUM, Dave Douglass presented the keynote speech.

> Climate camp's model of sustainability can appear as a holiday in scarcity to the casual observer

The Earth disnae give a bugger
– Dave Douglass

Douglass came across as humorous, thoughtful and angry, equally at home in both NUM and Climate Camp circles. In comparison to the other miners delegates his presentation was discursive and wide ranging. He admitted the human impact on climate change, but emphasised its natural movement, believing that natural factors are more likely to wipe out humanity, or even asteroids from space. In this he was ducking the issue since the issue is not so much whether climate change is 'natural' or 'man made' as the effect of a particular social relation, capitalism, on the way humanity interacts with the environment.[4]

He was on stronger ground when he argued that there was a reification of climate change that came out of a green view of nature: 'As a painted landscape pantomime at the Theatre Royal.' Nature, rather than being an abstraction, was always linked to the productive activity of humanity, the Earth as a 'dead crust' rather than some Gaia like entity. For myself, viewing the earth as a 'dead crust' ends up as much of a reification as environmentalist visions of Gaia. The productive activity that links humanity with nature is never simply exerted upon something inert – a 'dead crust' is as much of an abstraction as Gaia, both remaining within the logic of capital. The necessity was to address climate change from the perspective of the poor and exploited. Capitalism was incapable of doing so, but some trade unions like the NUM and IWW had this perspective. Renewables were fine but not wind farms, partly because they desecrated open spaces. He called for fair trade coal as a way of both invigorating the UK coal industry and addressing exploitation abroad. Douglass also emphasised the running down of the UK mining industry for political reasons, accusing the green movement of complicity with this process.

> **The class tensions around Climate Camp seemed like a clash of cultures**

Environmentalism and Climate Camp undoubtedly attract a lot of green mystical cretinism, but Douglass' ire was misdirected in terms of the environmentalists present, all being scrupulously materialist in their thinking on climate change. Stressing the natural cycle of climate change meant that Douglass actually made more of Nature than they did.

Douglass also introduced a topic that other NUM speakers emphasised: the industrial working class, in this case miners, have an inherent political perspective and class consciousness lacking in the service industries. It's certainly impossible to imagine mass pickets of Pret A Manger workers confronting cops, although that would be quite an event. But it's equally impossible to (re)posit the mass worker as the vanguard of class consciousness, since the conditions for that kind of organisation no longer exist in the UK. Context changes all, and it is sobering to realise that whereas 10,000 miners confronted cops at Orgreave in 1984, there are now around 5,000 miners in total. A workerist ideology introduces nostalgia rather than facing the reality of disseminated struggles against capitalism that elements of Climate Camp arise out of.

Other NUM delegates were more narrowly focused upon clean coal as a tech-

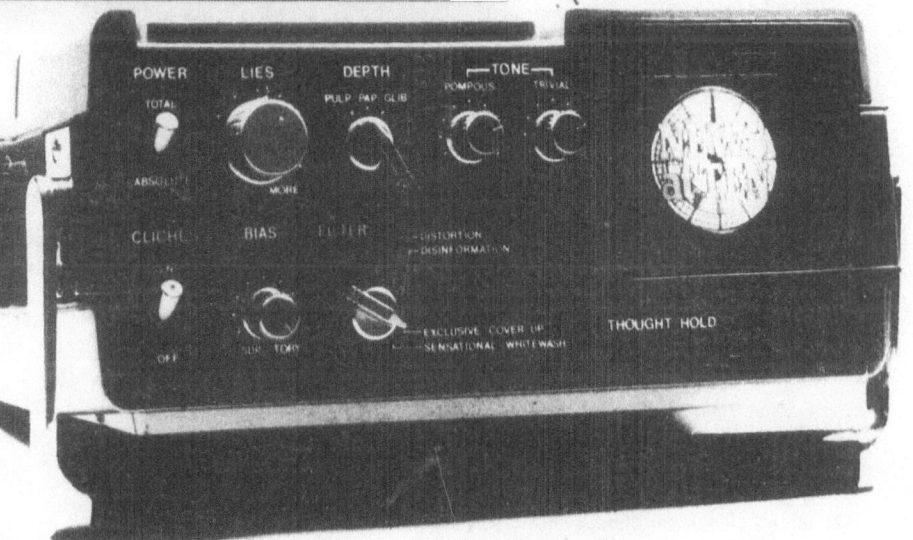

Image: Dave Douglass, *Tell Us Lies About the Miners*, 1985 (pamphlet cover)

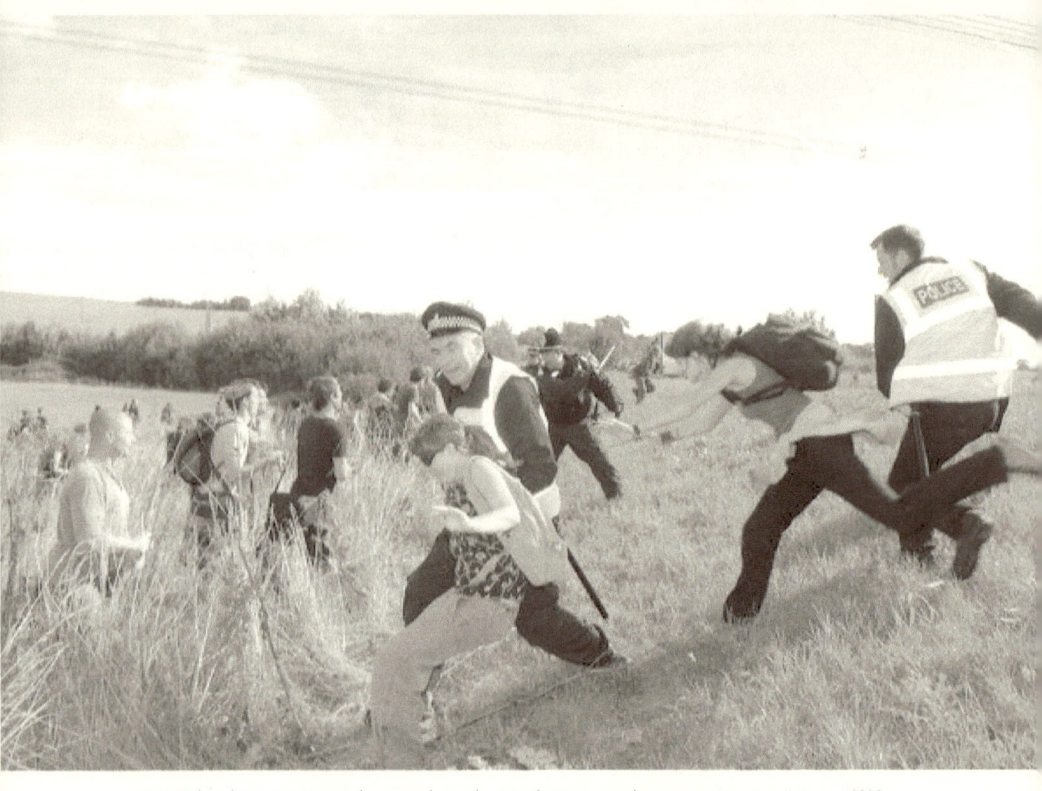

Image: Police chase environmental activists during the assault on Kingsnorth power station, Kent, 9 August 2008

nological solution to climate change, the continued viability of carbon-based industry and the future of mining communities. Scargill's presentation followed the oratorical model of old style trade unionism, with Arthur standing up and lots of gesticulation and pointing. Speaking loudly he could have been addressing the Durham Big Meeting. He made a well researched, belligerent case for the continued relevance of coal to energy policy, packing his speech with statistics and questioning the emphasis upon coal as a cause of global warming, a point echoed by other NUM speakers. Scargill went on for twice the 20 minutes allotted, in true leftist style, with everyone from the chairman onwards probably too overawed/exhausted to intervene. Scargill left soon after.

All of the Climate Campers were at pains to emphasise that they were not hostile to mining communities and were aware of the intrinsic relationship between climate change, class exploitation and capitalism. They also all underlined that they were not 'official' representatives of Climate Camp. This was undoubtedly one of the lines that separated the trade unionists from the Climate Campers, the union officials having a much more unproblematic relation to being a representative of the working classes. The Climate Campers were definitely from the more anti-capitalist wing and it might have been interesting had someone from a more single-issue perspective been present. Paul Chatterton, activist and Leeds

University academic, gave a well reasoned presentation about the need for a 'just transition'. After underlining the importance of avoiding a climate change 'tipping point' of a four degrees rise, he emphasised that environmentally based politics were ultimately against 'mindless, ceaseless growth' in the form of neoliberal capitalism. 'Just transition' would share out the costs of climate change equally, through a 'green new deal', ecological Keynesianism creating a 'green collar economy'. This would amount to the re-nationalisation of energy production and a rejection of the market.

I must admit that the concept of a 'green new deal' makes me want to strangle the planet with a couple of spare plastic bags. It's the realist corollary to the utopian elements of Climate Camp, but such an uncritical acceptance of a social democratic solution ignores the problem that capitalist social relations would still remain in place. It would be compatible with the development of an authoritarian, biopolitical state, obsessed with the administration of life. It is quite easy to imagine a dystopian 'green new deal' that continued the valorisation of capital alongside a work-ethic based morality all too conducive to the more sanctimonious elements of environmentalism. Chatterton did mention that a 'green new deal' might lead to less work and more holidays, a rare acknowledgement that climate change might not necessitate new regimes of scarcity. There is in this a trace of what was missing in the conference, a sense of possibility not embedded in soft focus 'somewhere else' utopianism but in an immanent engagement with capital's apparatus of capture. However, a 'green new deal' is unlikely to deliver the kind of simultaneous refusal of scarcity and production that might begin to construct a genuine anticapitalist response to the exigencies of climate change. It hardly amounts to a critique of wage labour.

Ian Lavery, President of the NUM, underlined the gulf between the NUM and Climate Campers through his refusal to engage with Paul Chatterton's case for 'just transition'. Remarking dismissively that he was in the bar during

The Earth disnae give a bugger

A Climatic Disorder? Class, Coal and Climate Change

Chatterton's talk, apparently what was needed was a 'just transition' to clean coal. Throughout the conference the NUM's concentration upon clean coal raised questions about the contradiction of trade unions being not only a bureaucratic appendage to the marketing of labour but also a possible focal point for resistance and the reproduction of communities tied to a particular industry. Lavery's work ethic was committed to coal rather than a green collar economy. He left shortly afterwards in his big car to go to another meeting. Oh, the life of the full time official.

The focus on new technologies as a general fix for climate change always threatens to introduce a Hollywood blockbuster narrative: 'And then there was clean coal...' While the viability of clean coal is in doubt, any present development of it is reliant upon capital being able to extract value from it.[5] The same would go for the development of renewables. It is unlikely that an exclusive focus on technology can really challenge the relation between climate change and the reproduction of capitalism.

David Guy, President of the North East area of the NUM, made a restrained and dignified argument for the viability of the North East Coalfield and spoke with some melancholy of the effects of the post-1984 strike on what used to be the 'left wing juggernaut' of the trade union movement. He pointed out that six months after the strike in 1985, and again in 1987, miners were back out on strike. A good reminder of how the memory of past struggle informs the present dilemma of the NUM, mining and ex-mining communities.

The next Climate Camper was Paul Morrozo, who made the connection between climate change and hurricane Katrina, pointing out that it was the precarious poor who suffered while the rich escaped, as demonstrated by the wholesale privatisation and gentrification of New Orleans. He also pointed out that climate change would put a squeeze on capitalism's attempts to avoid financial crisis and, I would add, its attempts to address climate change. More workers control was essential to combat climate change. He was willing to countenance mining if carbon capture was developed as a transitional measure, but argued that it was still in an experimental phase; the state and E.on were both lying about Kingsnorth's potential for carbon capture. Ultimately, if resources continue to be extracted, 'we're toast'.

Morrozo's contribution was constantly interrupted by the chairman, NUM official Dave Hopper, resplendent in both red shirt and red tie in case we didn't get the message. Hopper seemed to take great offence at any anti-coal argument, cutting in at one point with 'Put one of those windmills on your head and walk around with it'. This might have been funny to him but most objected strongly, especially when he seemed to have a fit after being heckled by a woman. At this point he resigned to be replaced by Dave Douglass. This was one of the few

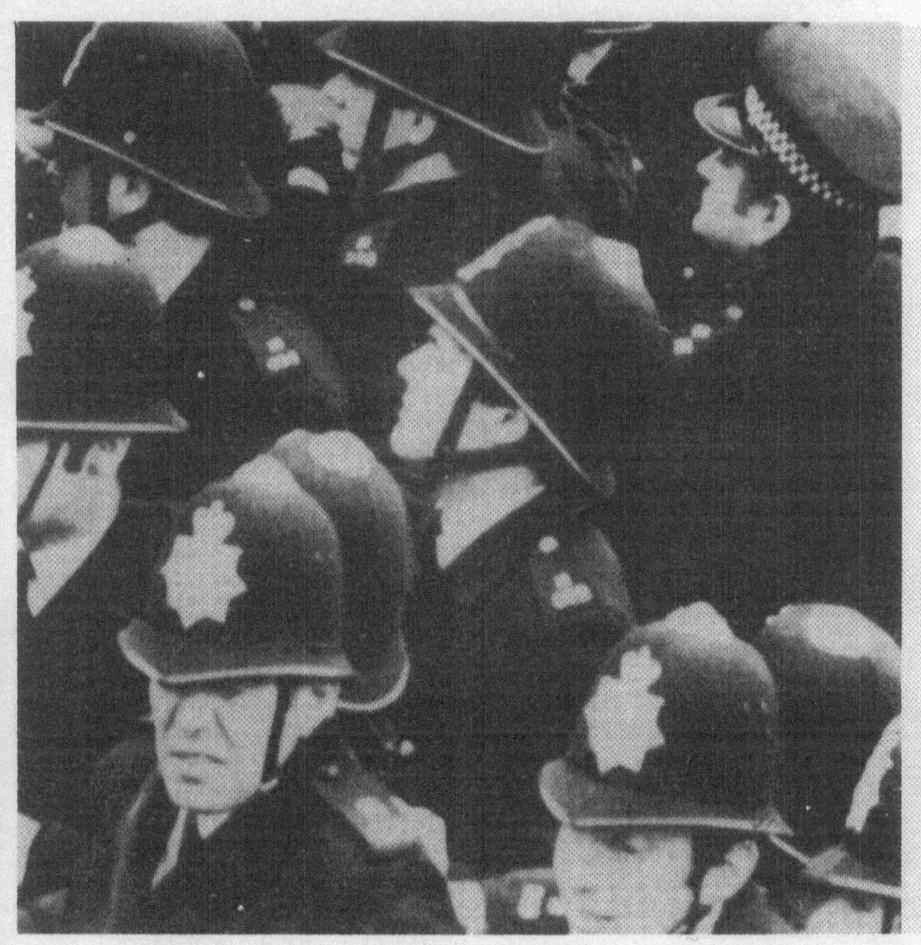

Image: Dave Douglass, Come and Wet this Truncheon, 1986 (pamphlet cover)

points at which a residual animosity surfaced, the atmosphere generally being more constructive.

The RMT regional secretary Stan Herschel spoke on the influence of the road lobby and the confluence of interests in business that work against environmentally sustainable energy resources and the trade union movement. At this point I must admit my mind was drifting towards a pint and my own most sustainable way home.

The last speaker was Kevin Bland of Green Anarchism, who talked about the class nature of climate change as the poor carry the cost, a point NUM delegates had also made. He was against the continued mining of coal and questioned the environmental credentials of carbon capture. Open cast mining was unacceptable and a form of revenge on mining communities. His description of the work done by local environmental groups against opencast suggested to me a much more investigative and open process than much of the Climate Camp activists' grandstanding, since it involved the self-organisation of communities. Class emerged as less of an abstraction here than in other eco-activists' presentations. He was also surprisingly sympathetic to Douglass' class analysis of Climate Camp, describing many supporters as weekend hippies but stressed that many did not fit this description. There was a suggestion by an NUM delegate that the union might be prepared to pursue an anti-opencast collaboration with environmentalists, as it had with 'No Opencast' in the 1990s.[6] There was also a lot of general debate between the various presentations, my favourite contribution being a sort of ode to coal as alchemical material by a retired miner, thanking it for the gift of class struggle.

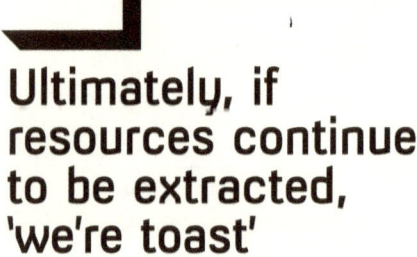

Ultimately, if resources continue to be extracted, 'we're toast'

The conference often threatened to become nothing but the conjunction of two forms of reformism – trade unionism and environmentalism – disputing the response to climate change rather than providing a challenge to the commodification of the world that both climate change and capital are predicated upon. Both trade unionists and activists discussed climate change and class as though they were only connected when the poor, or a particular segment of the working class, were victims of disaster or a shift in production, necessitating the intervention of a union or activist community.

Beyond the stereotypes of pit helmets and dreadlocks the central questions the conference raised for me are how to formulate a response to climate change capable of resisting capital's own one – given that capitalism loves a good catastrophe from which to extract value. Is there an inherent connection between capital, disaster and labour? In 1951, Italian ultra-leftist Amadeo Bordiga drew on Marx's concept of 'dead labour' (past labour solidified in the infrastructure it has produced) to demonstrate why capitalism is 'the masterful development of an economy based on disasters'.[7] In his words,

> To exploit living labour, capital must destroy dead labour which is still useful. Loving to suck young warm blood it kills corpses.[8]

His point was that capital thrived on disaster because it provided the opportunity to extract more surplus value from living labour through production. Bordiga suggests in this way that disaster, capital and labour are imbricated – class and labour rather than being a factor to consider in the disaster of climate change are central to it. Climate change often seems to be the product of two inhuman agencies, nature and capitalism, but it's unlikely that a return to trade union forms of organisation, even 'one big union', could produce the necessary oppositional force to counter this. Despite the tensions within the conference, I felt it was constructive in beginning to open a dialogue around this issue: what forms of class composition and organisation might arise within a climate change paradigm dominated by an increasingly authoritarian state and capital's need to prosper?

Info

The Labour Movement Conference 'Class, Climate Change and Clean Coal – the Climate Campers and the Unions' was held at the Bridge Hotel in Newcastle Upon Tyne, 1 November 2008

Footnote

[1] *Climate Camp Newspaper*, August 2008 – copies can be obtained at, networking@climatecamp.org.uk
[2] Dave Douglass, Climate Camp report, http://www.indymedia.org.uk/en/2008/08/407011.html
[3] See *Techno-Fixes: A critical guide to climate change technologies*, Corporate Watch report, 2008 pp.35-39, for more on carbon storage, http://www.corporatewatch.org
[4] Will Barnes, 'Capital Climes', Mute Vol 2 #5, 2007, http://www.metamute.org/en/Capital-Climes
[5] 'Techno-fixes', op.cit.
[6] See *Do Or Die*, issue 7, pp.23-32, for details on this campaign, http://www.eco-action.org/dod/no7/23-32.html
[7] 'Murdering the Dead', Amadeo Bordiga, p.31, Antagonism Press, 2000.
[8] Ibid, p.36.

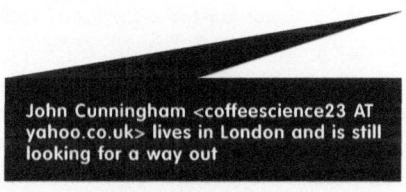

John Cunningham <coffeescience23 AT yahoo.co.uk> lives in London and is still looking for a way out

LIVERPOOL – CULTURE OF CAPITAL

Reporting on the conference Capital, Culture and Power in Liverpool, Leo Singer and Clara Paillard crash the regeneration party and pose some difficult questions for its hosts

– Stuck in its glare we lose sight of structure
Roy Coleman speaking of Liverpool's urban patriotism

For three days in July, Liverpool University and Liverpool John Moores University hosted a critical conference about urban regeneration in Liverpool. Both its size and the high proportion of activists present were unusual for an academic conference. Of 155 participants nearly half were non-academics: community activists, community workers, artists and working class activists.

The conference was organised by the European Group for the Study of Deviance and Social Control, an association of radical sociologists and criminologists. In the middle of Liverpool's year as European Capital of Culture, the organisers decided to devote much of the conference programme to dissenting voices.

The city has recently been submerged under an avalanche of discourse dealing with our everyday lives. The 'creative industries' (including the art house cinema, art galleries, and local media) have been especially active in the field of ideological production. They have been commissioned to deliver various cross-class messages to the city residents. FACT (Foundation for Art and Creative Technology) and Radio BBC Merseyside were asking questions such as: Where are 'we' going to? Who are 'we'? Are 'we' more free than 'we' think? Where are the boundaries of 'our' bodies? What is the identity of this city?, etc. Discourses celebrating the new, post-industrial and cosmopolitan 'community' subtly sweep away the outdated *Boys From The Black Stuff*-like traditions and any sources of identity coming from the working class world.

A number of readily available and servile 'creatives' ensure that the ideological production of the ruling class is sold to traditionally suspicious Scousers in a non-intrusive and 'cool' way. Various dialogical, participatory, experiential platforms, venues and projects have been developed to achieve this task.

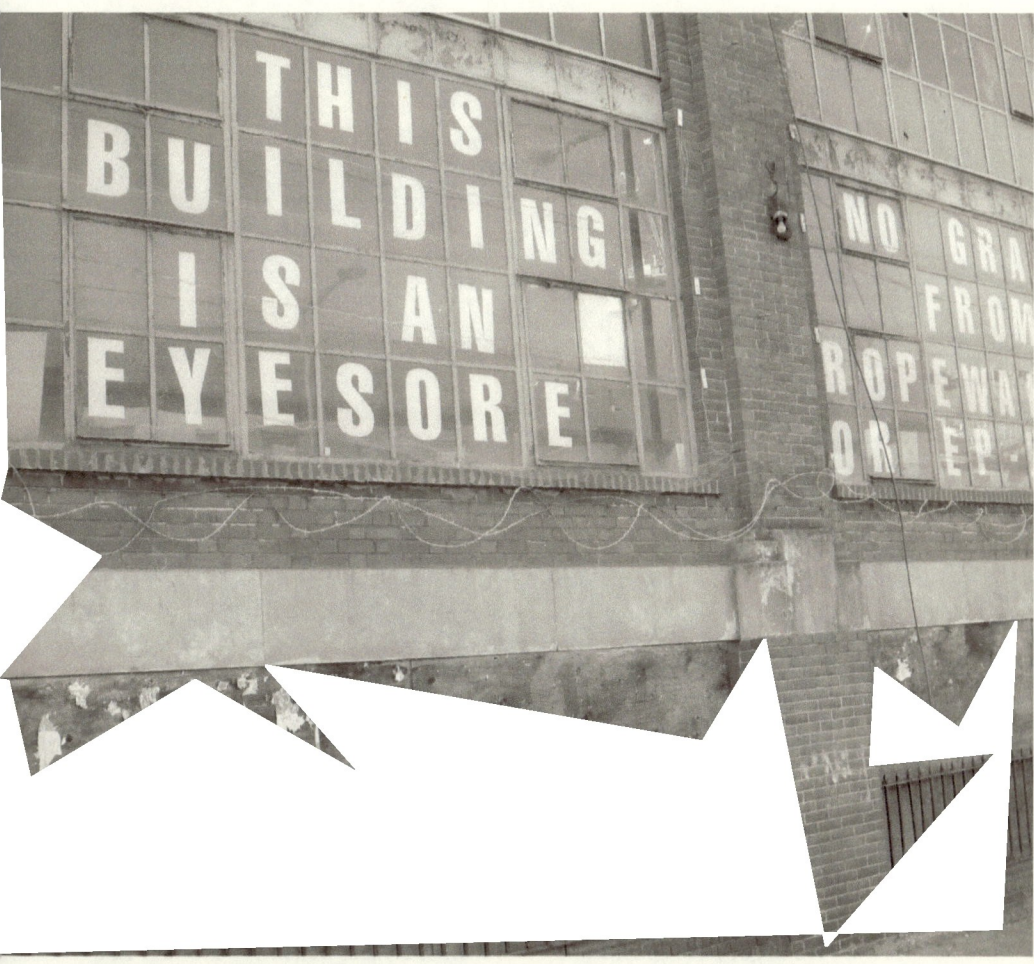

Image: Anti-regeneration in Liverpool's Chinatown. All photographs by Leo Singer and Clara Paillard

Mutant Patriotism

One example of how cynical inhabitants are turned into participants in the year-long cultural party is the Super Lamb Banana phenomenon. The original work by the Japanese artist Taro Chiezo, commissioned for the Art Transpennine Exhibition in 1998, was conceived as a protest against genetically modified food. The Super Lamb Banana is, as the name suggests, a heroic composite of lamb and banana, a reference to Liverpool's history of exporting lamb and importing bananas. The City of Culture grasped the potential of this piece of public art and turned it into a symbol of Liverpudlian 'wackiness', thus packaging all sorts of stereotypes about Scousers into a much-celebrated commodity. *The Liverpool Echo* is exemplary in whipping up this kind of hysteria. One of the top articles recently reported on a group of local scouts

Liverpool – Culture of Capital

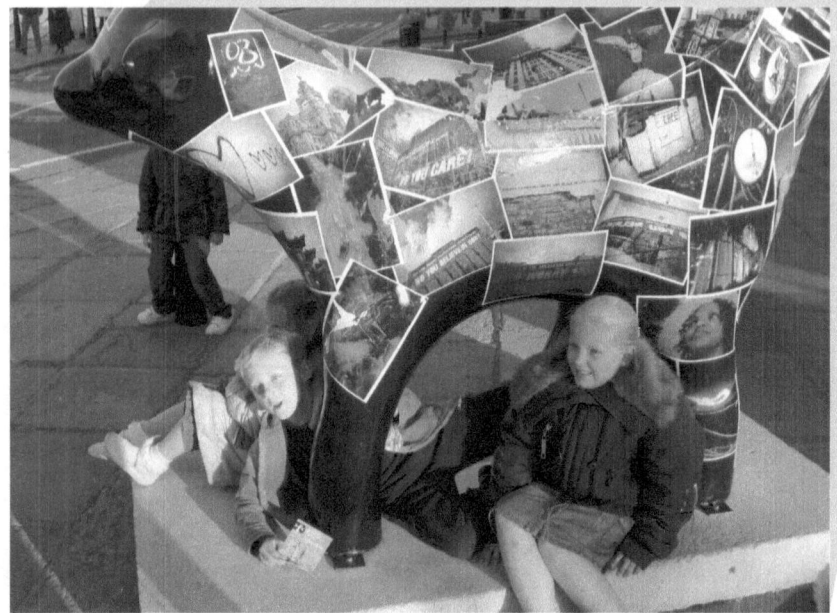

Image: One of the many miniature replicas of Taro Chiezo's *Super Lamb Banana*

who within 24 hours managed to visit all 200-plus Lamb Banana statues scattered over the city! As the scout leader put it:

> We've got photographs of every Superlambanana we visited and we're now trying to register the attempt with the Guinness Book of Records and hope it will be made into an official record.

And by the way, the *Echo*'s article makes sure that every reader gets the message that this Super Lamb Banana hunt was sponsored by the companies Honda, Barclays, BBA Aviation and the city's Comet stores...

Experiencing the Lamb Banana hysteria, one immediately understands the concept of urban patriotism, introduced by Roy Coleman during his keynote speech at the conference. He defined urban patriotism as a strategy of rule for regeneration managers that appears apolitical, banal and funny, thus mystifying class relations. Like all forms of patriotism this kind is narrow-minded, focused on simple images, emotive, celebratory in nature and lacking in reasoning. It is organised around a kind of pride and a 'love' of consumption, 'heritage', iconic buildings or objects like the Lamb Bananas, etc. And like the national variety, urban patriotism glosses over and deflects attention from the less glamorous aspects of regeneration, including class division, continuing poverty and marginalisation of communities. Coleman continues: 'It involves universities, political decision-

35 percent of city centre apartments were vacant even pre-credit crunch

making, marketing, retail sector, policing'. Despite the bombastic and self-confident language employed in this strategy, it is a sign of both the incapacity to face up to reality and 'a means of defence against those deemed to undermine "the brand" or the strategy'.

Bubble Economics

Private developers and speculators have been playing the regeneration game for years in Liverpool. But it is important not to lose sight of the fact that the bulk of city regeneration has been financed from public sources (EU Objectives 1 and 2, governmental subsidies, New Deal for Communities, etc.) The major private investment is the £1 billion Liverpool One Project, probably the largest single private development in Europe funded by big retail money. This 42.5 acre shopping site in the heart of the city – policed by private security and omnipresent CCTV cameras – was described as a 'retail republic' in a *Guardian* article from May this year.

Stuart Wilks-Heeg's (University of Liverpool) myth-busting analysis showed that the growth of the city in the last 10 years was not driven by the new economy but rather by the expansion of the public sector (65 percent net job growth). Since 1997, 10,000 manufacturing jobs were lost and 14,000 new jobs in the service economy (call centres) were created. Real unemployment is still around 15-25 percent and the level of skills among workers remains very low. The vulnerability of capital's composition in Liverpool lies in its reliance on public subsidy and cheap credit to sustain the local housing market and construction. So, with 35 percent of city centre apartments vacant even before the credit crunch and the new Liverpool One opening just at the moment that a sharp drop of consumer spending is expected, where is the city heading?

Cue the Quangos

Liverpool has become the theatre for the worst comedy of the century, with luxury flats germinating like weeds and shopping malls flourishing on any land that's grab-able. But behind the private sector's iconic absurdities hide a myriad of semi-public agencies, populating the local political space at great speed. One after another they usurp the stage of local democracy, pushing out elected representatives and local citizens. This new theatrical

Liverpool – Culture of Capital

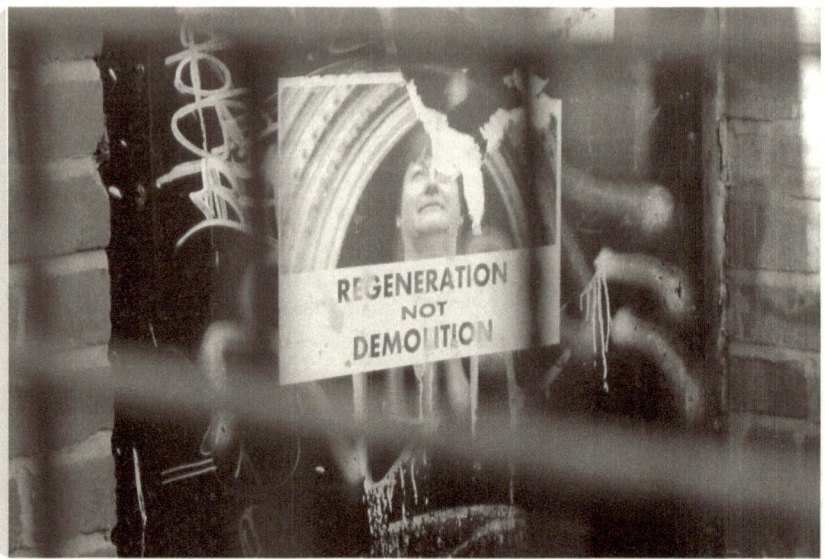

Image: Poster featuring OAP Elizabeth Pascoe who successfully claimed that a compulsory purchase order forcing her to leave her home in Adderley Street breached her human rights, thus delaying an English Partnership project to demolish 500 homes in the area to make way for a widened road into Liverpool city centre

troop are faithful to the Thatcherite script, albeit in a version reanimated by New Labour and its prophets.

The first quango to appear in Liverpool was the Merseyside Development Corporation (MDC), established after the Toxteth uprising in 1981. The MDC was put in charge of regenerating the Albert Dock, the so-called 'jewel in the crown' of Liverpool's 'renaissance'. The Blair era produced new characters to enrich the local 'quangocracy' with the North West Development Agency (NWDA) set up to help create an environment in which businesses in the region could flourish.

Liverpool relies on public subsidy and cheap credit for housing

This was soon followed by its offspring, Liverpool Vision, an urban regeneration company created to transform the city into one of the UK's leading business destinations by means of an ambitious and far-reaching regeneration programme. Kensington Regeneration, a quango set up to invest in the working class area of Kensington, was funded by the New Deal for Communities. This programme was launched in 1998 as a key part of the Government's strategy for 'regeneration in the

39 most deprived areas across the country'. The package for Liverpool is £62 million. And last but not least the Housing Market Renewal Initiative (HMRI) arrived to deliver the final blow to local inhabitants in other neighbourhoods. Today the stage is crowded with these quangos, disguised as community initiatives and local projects.

But what has been done for the people of Liverpool? Gentrifying the inner city with bulldozers? Redesigning entire communities? Spending millions on 'culture' to allow the high-flyers of the hospitality industry to enter the city? Selling public land to property developers? The North West Development Agency (NWDA) subsidises private profit by handing huge sums of money to speculators. In Kensington, entire Victorian streets are being demolished to allow land assembly to operate in favour of developers.[1] People are being evicted without discrimination from both social and private housing by the New Deal. In the city centre, Liverpool Vision has sold the waterfront to any developers able to build over twelve storeys and has made helping the private sector fill its pockets a priority, just in time for the present 'crisis'.

Spoiling the Party

Generally, urban regeneration is led by a forced and false consensus rather than public debate, to the point where there is little discernible difference between marketing and public consultation processes. A key issue at the conference was how policy-driven research is incorporating academics, promoting the selective adoption of academic arguments and the misuse of public consultation.

A prime example remains the saga of the 'Fourth Grace'. A 'tall iconic building capable of attracting more visitors to the city and based on Liverpool's culture and history' was supposed to complement the famous Three Graces – industrial skyscrapers erected to celebrate the city's boom a hundred years ago. A public exhibition was held in 2002 to give the public a chance to have their say about the design. Four projects were presented in a catwalk fashion with models and 3D fly-through visualisations. Visitors were asked to 'vote' for their preferred scheme. When Liverpool Vision's decision was announced, the whole city was stunned: they had chosen the least popular building to be built on the waterfront. However, after two years of public spending to promote it, the project collapsed in 2004.

In this concert of demagogy and commodification, activist voices can rarely be heard. Fortunately, they could at the conference. *Nerve* magazine, promoting grassroots culture and organising in Merseyside, hosted a session where residents gave their accounts of the hidden face of the Capital of Culture mega-party.

Hazel and Stella from the Granby Triangle testified to the 'lie of consultation' that led to the decision to demolish hundreds of homes in their area:

> All what they could ask was 'What sort of houses do you want?' and we kept saying 'the ones we are in now', they never listened.

Their homes are earmarked for a 'regeneration' scheme that will demolish perfectly good Victorian and Georgian houses to make way for new developments that are unlikely to last more than half a century.

Nina Edge, who lives in the 'Welsh Streets' area in Toxteth, told the story of her community of South Liverpool:

> On one side of the road, the houses are branded 'Victorian 5-bed houses with view on Princes Park' and are valued at £350,000 and on the other side, they are 'derelict dwellings unfit for habitation' and owners are offered £60,000 for them, how is that?

Elisabeth Pascoe, a campaigner from Edge Lane, is still fighting tooth and nail against the Compulsory Purchase Order (CPO) imposed on her house and those of hundreds of other people in her community. The use of CPOs (based on the 1993 Housing and Urban Development Act) means mobilising the State's brutal powers – originally designed to provide for the re-use of brownfield areas – against a poor community. Pascoe warns that this sets an important precedent relevant to residents in housing areas all over the country.

People in the affected communities have been put under stress and troubling rates of mortality have been observed in these areas (33 people in Edge Lane and 9 in the Welsh Streets). Rather than helping local people get a better place to live, the master planners have bulldozed and divided local neighbourhoods. But local people are fighting back and by the end of the conference a support network had been set up bringing together local residents and researchers for the first time.

While it is true that local people have been organising against the demolition of homes, and to protect local heritage and parks, the opposition has been fragmented, often focusing on individual issues rather than linking together. The strong presence of activists and working class people at the conference would probably not have been possible without the effort and authority of the *Nerve*. During a period marked by the relative absence of visible class struggles in this dormant, formerly radical city, the magazine has served as a link between area-based groups, un-organised left-wing individuals, artists and academics. It is a rallying point for people with experience of different political generations and movements: the mass workers' struggles in the

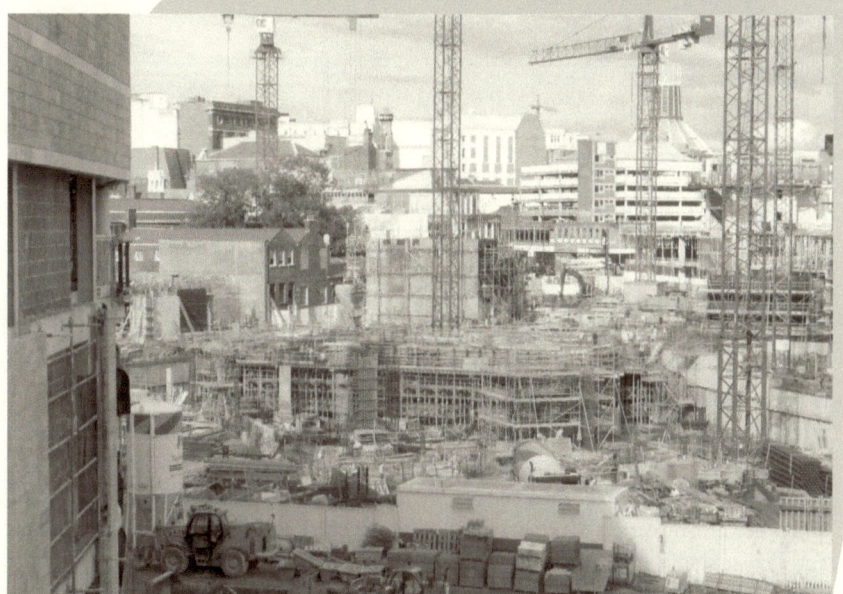

Image: Construction of Liverpool One shopping and leisure district. One of these cranes, the property of Norfolk based Falcon Crane Hire company, collapsed in January 2007, killing a Polish worker, Zbigniew Swirzinski. Since he was self-employed and working without a contract his family hasn't received any compensation. Families Against Corporate Killers (FACK) are demanding a more just investigation. Meanwhile, the same type of crane remains in use

1970s, the unemployed youth and squatters' movement in the 1980s, and a more diverse spectrum of social struggles (including anti-regeneration campaigns) from the 1990s on.

The Role of the University Revisited

The conference was an important statement against the self-congratulatory City of Culture rhetoric. It is a paradox that a radical conference was hosted by two universities which are key partners in Liverpool Vision as well as owners and developers of important properties in the city centre. The universities serve as an informal think tank for the City of Culture project. Only a few metres from the conference rooms, a team of sociologists commissioned by the City Council and Liverpool Culture Company were working on their research on regeneration. This project, 'Impacts 08', has had little impact on the regeneration debate other than to support its marketing strategy.

We pointed out this split among academics to sociologist David Whyte, one of the conference organisers, who outlined a complex picture of the role of universities today. He argued that they are neither autonomous spaces of open free discussion nor uniform knowledge factories producing analysis for the State or private sector companies. They are rather terrains of constant struggle where the attachment to academic freedom can still provide cover for radical research. For Whyte, academics often exaggerate the oppressiveness of university commodification in order to justify their passivity and pursuit of government grants. Neoliberalism does exert disciplining pressure but university workers still can organise against that:

> The fact that critical work emerges from university ground is not a function of the institution itself. It is always a result of struggles that create the space for this work.

Some of the organisers conceived the conference as an opportunity to build up links with working class and social movements. It is questionable to what extent this was achieved. In November 2008 Liverpool's new BT Convention Centre will be the venue for a conference on the city's regeneration entitled 'On the Waterfront'. Sponsored by the city, the quangos and (surprisingly?) Liverpool University, anyone who wants to get into this event will have to pay £250. Of course no potential troublemaker has been invited to this 'intellectual' celebration of policy makers, developers, consultants and other urban patriots. Compared to this event, the Conference on Capital, Culture and Power stands out as a far more democratic enterprise. No entry fees, free food and drinks at a party in the university atrium, and friendly debates regardless of 'who is who'.

On the other hand, the conference 'on Capital' did not really deepen our understanding of how workers, to whom the academics want to relate, produce capital in their everyday lives. Some of the organisers – Gramscian Marxist sociologists – research conditions of work on construction sites in Liverpool city centre and support campaigning families of workers killed at work. But their serious activity can't replace our research into other related questions. What is the class composition of the new industries or 'upgraded' areas? What strategies do call centre, restaurant, or shop workers use to cope with the demands of their bosses or clients? Are there any experiences of or possibilities for struggle here? One can dismiss these questions claiming that 'the conference wasn't about that.' But this is exactly the problem.

New Labour's urban policy project is about delivery of public resources to private projects. To sustain this sophisticated managerial operation the State needs to generate a highly complex web of governance mechanisms. It is exactly here that the plethora of quangos and 'community empowerment' programmes with their own circular languages are located. It seems that most critical academic research follows this moving target, shifting attention away from something more fundamental – the transformation of work in a 'booming' city and how this feeds the drive of capital.

If the academics who participated in the conference want to demonstrate a commitment to the working class, they should spend less time confronting New Labour's urban policies, various local hegemonies and quangos and instead turn toward the everyday processes of the constitution of work. Because, while some of us may become victims of urban regeneration or crime in our neighbourhoods, all of us have to sell our labour power in one form or another.

Leo Singer and Clara Paillard

Info

Capital, Culture, Power: Criminalisation and Resistance was hosted by the University of Liverpool and Liverpool John Moores University on behalf of the British-Irish Section of the European Group for the Study of Deviance and Social Control, 2-4 July, 2008

Footnote

1 Land assembly is a term used in planning to explain the activity of planners and/or professionals who seek to bring together small parcels of land (private and/or public) to create a larger parcel. This is an exercise often used to provide more space for large-scale urban projects (public or private). Sometimes the public sector can seek land assembly to build public facilities but at the moment it merely provides land to housing developers to create large private housing developments for maximum profit.

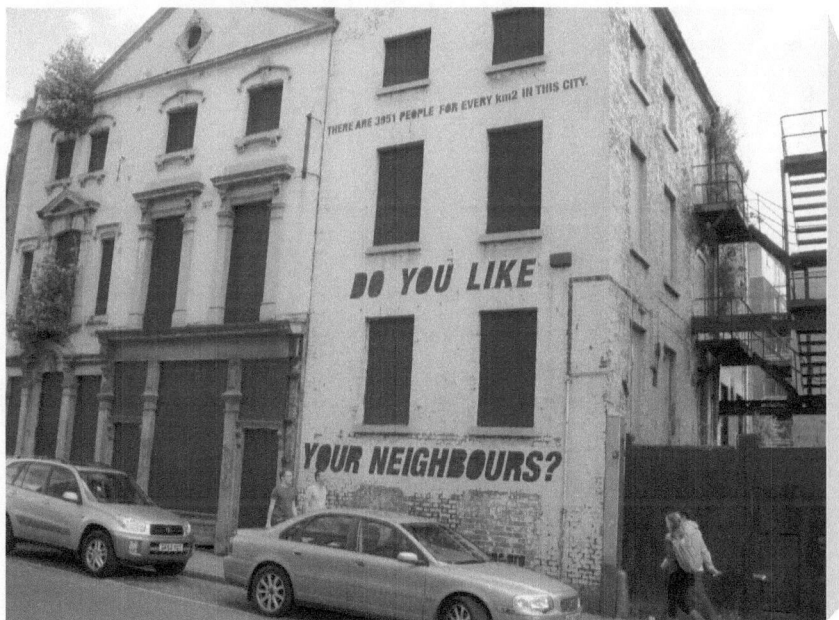

Image: Stockholm artists collective A-APE' s interventions on walls in the city centre. Project commissioned by the Liverpool Culture Company as part of European Capital of Culture 2008 and managed by Liverpool Biennial

Leo Singer is a community worker and a drop in the new East European migrant 'wave' to the UK. Together with Clara Paillard, as part of a larger research group, he is researching the class composition of the hospitality sector in Liverpool's city centre

Clara Paillard <c.paillard@liv.ac.uk> is a French political activist and member of the Campaign for a New Workers' Party. She is completing her PhD on urban regeneration and democracy at University of Liverpool. Clara coordinates an Alternative Programme to the Capital of Culture '08. More info at: www.myspace.com/cityofculture08

TAKE ME I'M YOURS: NEOLIBERALISING THE CULTURAL INSTITUTION

While talk of precariousness is rife in cultural and political forums, 'progressive' institutions do not always practice what they preach. Anthony Davies looks behind the scenes of 'radical reformism'

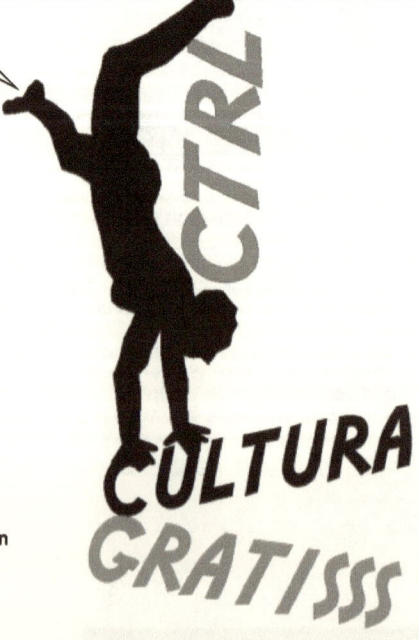

Anthony Davies

In March 2006, the Museum of Contemporary Art, Barcelona (MACBA), flagship 'progressive art institution', staged the second part of Another Relationality, a conference and workshop project examining the legacy of institutional critique and the new social and political functions of art. The event included presentations from sociologist Maurizio Lazzarato, critic-activist Brian Holmes and economist Antonella Corsani – all broadly associated with debates on the role of creativity, knowledge and subjectivity within contemporary capitalism.

Just prior to a conference workshop in which they had been invited to participate, local activist collective ctrl-i issued a public declaration of withdrawal, accusing the museum of complicity with the very neoliberal imperatives it purported to critique. On the surface at least, their statement – including the trenchant line 'Talking about precariousness in the McBa is like taking a nutrition seminar at McDonald's' – had the hallmarks of a typical struggle against institutionalisation. But there was one key difference: ctrl-i is partly made up of temp workers formerly employed by the museum and not, as might be expected, an unaligned or 'autonomous' body resisting co-optation. It was moreover their knowledge and critique of precarious labour conditions and cultural neoliberalisation in Barcelona that was to form the basis of their contribution. The collective had been born in direct response to an earlier MACBA event, El Precariat Social Rebel, where, under the auspices of activist network The Chainworkers, they spoke out against the museum's dubious employment practices and later gave up their jobs in circumstances that remain largely unclear.[1] While

> **Talking about precariousness in the McBa is like taking a nutrition seminar at McDonald's**

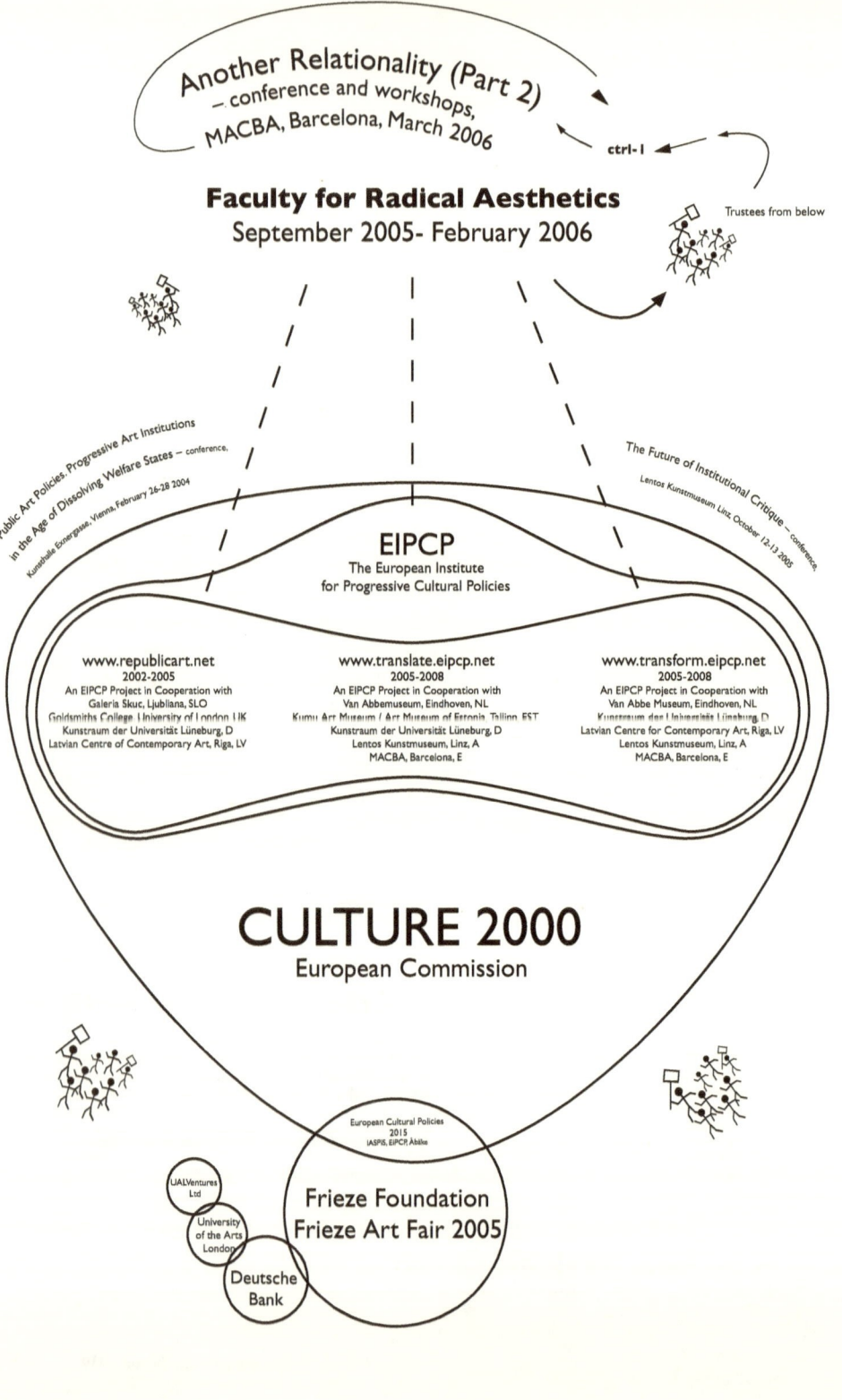

ctrl-i's unique status as temp workers and local activists may have prompted the invite from MACBA, it also gave the group licence to dramatise Another Relationality's underlying themes in an emphatic act of withdrawal.[2]

To understand the context for this signal act of protest on the part of a group of culture sector workers, and to give a material basis to the discussions on institutionalisation currently taking place in publications such as *Art Monthly* and *Mute*, we need first to look at the uneven process of neoliberal restructuring as it courses its way through cultural and educational institutions.[3] According to Marxist geographer David Harvey, neoliberalism's trademark rhetoric that human wellbeing is contingent on developing individual entrepreneurial freedoms – chiefly the freedom to operate in the market – should be contrasted with the unprecedented 'creative' destruction that accompanies neoliberal reform. In *A Brief History of Neoliberalism*, Harvey describes how this process results in an erosion of existing social relations, ways of life and thought, as the market gradually penetrates and puts to work the 'common sense' way that many of us live in and engage with the world. The state's role becomes principally that of ensuring the proper functioning of markets, setting up institutional frameworks which ultimately guarantee the 'maintenance, reconstitution and restoration of elite class power'. It is difficult to track these developments across different regional and national contexts, however, and this is exacerbated by the multifaceted, hybrid and localised manner in which they unfold, another symptom/condition of the process Harvey terms 'uneven geographical development'.[4]

Where do state-funded cultural and educational institutions fit into all this? What role do they play? At a point where many have been set to work by capital in ever more 'innovative' (read: commercialised) ways, a host of contradictions and antagonisms have surfaced. While some now openly promote the liberating capacity of new revenue streams linked to consultancy, outsourcing, business incubation and enterprise activities, others seek out more

---

Image: diagram by Nils Norman

tactical models of engagement, looking to new constituencies and standards of practice to offset the crisis of legitimation which opens up as institutions are subjected to neoliberal agendas.

An attempt to address some of these issues in the European cultural sector can be found in *European Cultural Policies 2015: A Report with Scenarios on the Future of Public Funding for Contemporary Art in Europe*.[5] This publication acted as the cornerstone of the International Artist Studio Program in Sweden's (Iaspis) contribution to the Frieze Art Fair, 2005. Against the backdrop of an earlier rejected proposal to the Frieze Foundation, state-funded Iaspis decided to pursue a more general enquiry into the cultural and political questions opened up by their compromised participation in the fair, focusing specifically on its exemplary and problematic identity as a 'public-private partnership'.[6] In collaboration with the European Institute for Progressive Cultural Policies (eipcp) and London-based design group Åbäke, Iaspis went on to commission reports from eight local experts on key social, political and economic determinants of cultural policy in seven regions across the EU. The reports integrated hypothetical scenarios of what the cultural landscape might look like in 2015 as well as introductions by Iaspis director Maria Lind and eipcp director Gerald Raunig. These latter two texts illustrate the grand ambitions of the project: to influence – and possibly reform – European cultural policy, and to strengthen 'radical-reformist elements of the cultural-political discourse in Europe'.[7]

In spite – or rather, because – of its political ambitions, *European Cultural Policies 2015*'s focus on the meshing of the state, its institutional apparatus, and the market elides any

> **European Cultural Policies 2015 elides any significant debate on class power within art institutions themselves**

Anthony Davies

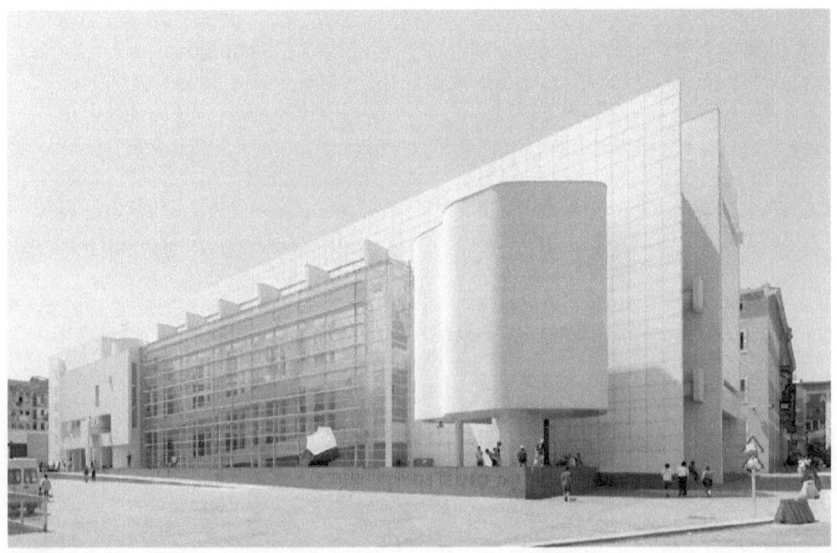

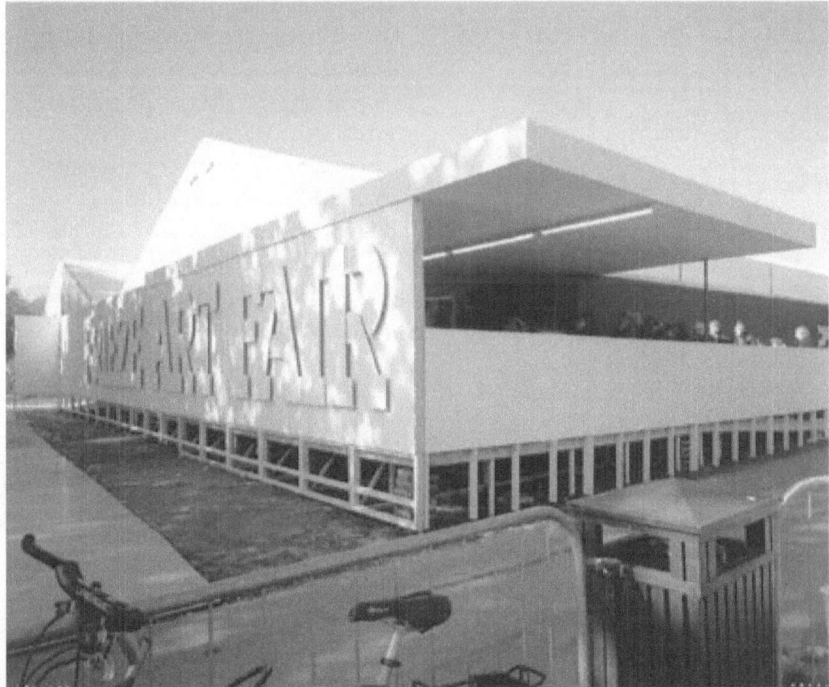

Image: Above, MACBA, Barcelona.
Below, Freize Art Fair, London.

significant debate on class power within art institutions themselves and across the commercial sectors with which they interact. This makes the underlying economic disparities and antagonisms associated with neoliberalism's specific mode of 'uneven development' impossible to gauge. It also obscures the interests of those whom the report's findings ultimately serve.

Along with the policy minutiae, however, we do get an insight into the inter-institutional faultlines opening up across Europe. The report's account of the breakdown of *Frieze*/Iaspis's earlier collaboration and the subsequent soul-searching undertaken by Iaspis director Maria Lind and her colleagues is symptomatic of such conflicts.

'Progressive' institutional voices, mostly those in the upper echelons (directors, key administrators and curators), in conjunction with a new type of defector academic/activist 'communication consultant to the prince' look for new operational models to open up a critical engagement with the institution's complicity in cultural neoliberalisation.[8] Lind's introduction to *2015* registers Iaspis's discomfort regarding the 'collaboration' with Frieze while the report itself atones by disclosing the financial details of the project. It's a characteristic deflective move. Frieze Art Fair's enthusiastic adoption of corporate values, dramatically high turnover and audience figures, together with the generally porous membrane separating its commercial and non-commercial activities, become the anti-model of neoliberal institutional practice, the vanguard of the 'almost completely instrumentalised' cultural/art dystopia for which we are notionally all destined in 2015.

The *2015* report contrasts this nightmare vision of neoliberal cultural lockdown with a wet dream of agile, socially responsible and responsive transnational infrastructures – something like eipcp's ever-expanding network of 'Co-organisers', 'Associated Partners', etc.[9] Behind its critical reflections on cultural policy there lies a bid for future state funding. The report's not so tacit conclusion is that the European Commission should

While affirming the fight against precarious labour, institutions continue to maintain high levels of labour insecurity among their workers

Anthony Davies

reconsider its priorities and shift monies away from the big players and richer member states (read: UK plc., Frieze & Co.) and over towards 'responsible actors' (read: Iaspis/eipcp) and smaller self-organising networks.

This goes some way to explaining the absence of any debate in the report on wage and labour relations within art institutions themselves. It also throws up other questions. For instance, given the EU's aim of promoting the transnational dissemination of culture as a catalyst for socio-economic development and social integration, and its funding of both Frieze and eipcp, which of the two operational models delivered the most 'European Added Value'?[10] The introduction to *2015* threw up a series of binaries: Iaspis-eipcp versus Frieze Art Fair; public versus public-private partnership; self-organised versus instrumentalised; institutions acting as 'responsible actors' versus institutions as mere 'facilitators'. However, these *alternatives* should not be read as divergent paths but as coexistent forms of neoliberalism, evolving at uneven rates and in different phases perhaps, but all moving in the same direction. Each leads towards the same future – one with a human face, the other without – as various institutional actors become the unacknowledged legislators of neoliberalism and work to pioneer a socially acceptable form of its hegemony.

This process sees a proliferation of transnational infrastructures connecting art institutions up with self-organised (activist) networks. As a tendency it can be tracked back at least as far as the earlier institutional incorporation of activist strategies in the late 1990s-early 2000s with MACBA frequently being cited as one of the first institutions to spearhead this with their Direct Action as One of the Fine Arts workshop in 2000 and Las Agencias (The Agencies) in mid 2001.[11] However, the consolidation of left radical-reformist agendas and coalitions at the first European Social Forum in Florence in

Image: MCBA Museum of
Contemporary Precarity Barcelona
subvertisement by CTRL-I
http://sindominio.net/ctrl-i

Take Me I'm Yours

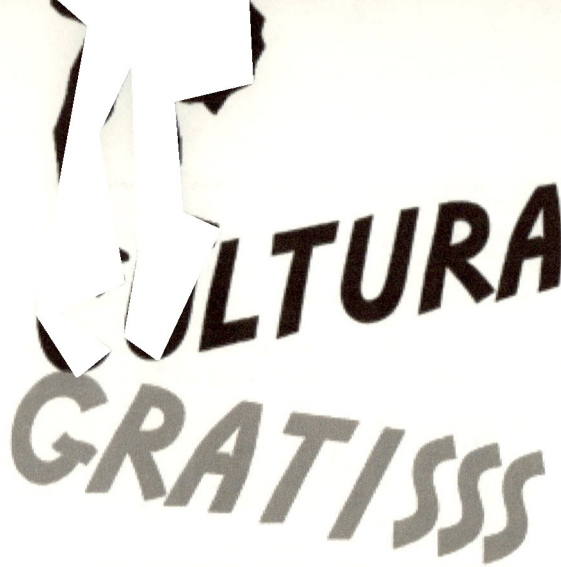

November 2002 provides the more obvious ideological blueprint for the type of 'critical' policy alternatives found in *2015*. Around this time, eipcp also launched its 'Republicart Manifesto', setting the tone and operational parameters of a three-year, EU-funded programme of events, web essays and conferences. This hauled a range of micro-institutional programmes and discourses into its investigation of the 'development of interventionist and activist practices of public art'. The manifesto also claimed to pose a corrective to the dialectical cul-de-sacs and 'revolutionary pathos' characterising '90s political art. It explicitly rejects 'reforming a form of state', but nevertheless lays out a road map that would later enable state-funded institutions to harness some of the provisional overlaps between their activities and those of social and political movements.[12]

Eipcp continues to function as the project leader in a transnational cartel of institutions and individuals, all of whom feed into its web portals *Republicart* (2002-05), *Transform (2005-2008)* and *Translate* (2005-), and back out, to conferences, symposia, exhibitions and workshops (see diagram). The network is now positioned at the institutional epicentre of a number of European cultural debates on progressive and radical reformist cultural strategies.

The phrase 'progressive art institution' for example can be tracked back to eipcp and, as a generalised catch-all, has proven itself particularly adaptable to the kind of concerted effort the network makes to generate a coherent theoretical framework. This project starts to take shape in the run up to the conference

Image: subvertisement by CTRL-I
http://sindominio.net/ctrl-i

Public Art Policies: Progressive Art Institutions in the Age of Dissolving Welfare States, in 2004. An open discussion on web platform Discordia between the organisers, participants and other interested parties offers an insight into some of the general confusion, disputes and problems associated with the term 'progressive'. According to eipcp's Raunig, it should be read as 'becoming' not 'being' progressive:

> this becoming progressive happens between the two poles of movement (micropolitical actions etc.) and institutions (political organisation, etc.). the abstract negation of one of these two poles would lead directly into myths of freedom (which I also suspect behind notions like 'open cultures' or 'free networks', especially if in connection to the art field) or reformist reductions.[13]

While key figures in the eipcp network continue to promote various modes of 'non-dialectical' engagement, any claims to new forms of resistance and political action should be tested by their effect on the core of the (art) institutions in question. If they simply serve to insulate and insure these neoliberal cultural nodes against attacks on their legitimacy or provide ideological cover for a process of economic restructuring, how 'progressive' are things becoming?

In addition to its pioneering approach to outsourcing, MACBA, according to its website, is economically supported by a foundation of thirty-eight sponsoring members and thirty-three founding businesses including multinational financial and consultancy services groups like Ernst and Young, Deloitte and scandal-hit Banco Bilbao Vizcaya Argentaria (BBVA).[14] As state-funded cultural and educational institutions pass through the eye of the neoliberal storm, it's hardly surprising that a conspicuous self-reflexivity about their inner contradictions has become the stock in trade of progressives and radical reformers alike, broadcasting consciousness of the problems but holding their resolution in abeyance. With uneven rates of movement and development between states, regions and cities, the institutions in which these professionals work are now bogged down in an erratic process of 'catch up' as the state at once withdraws public sector support and economically mobilises culture and education.

This can be seen in the plethora of strategies for public sector reform and outsourcing. On the one hand, new models of efficiency and standards of assessment are introduced, on the other institutions are given the task of attracting inward investment, contributing to cultural tourism, urban regeneration and the Creative Industries. Cultural and educational institutions, then, are in the midst of various forms of neoliberal enclosure and the concomitant restructuring is seen by competing individuals, networks and agencies to offer openings for a range of agendas seeking to gain purchase on institutional structures/bureaucracies. Referring to the market for higher education and universities for example, academic Ned Rossiter has argued that,

> just as NGOs and CSOs have filled the void created by the neoliberal state's evacuation from the social, so too must organised networks seize upon the institutional persona of the 'external provider'[15]

At the other end of the scale, the many and varied external providers linked to finance capital are also busy at work. At the inaugural conference of the British Venture Capital Association in September 2006, for example, companies referred to a 'land grab' as they rushed to secure stakes in the future output of university departments.[16] This activity is mirrored in the University of the Arts London's (UAL) Innovation Centre and wholly owned subsidiary company UALVentures – part of a dozen or so other schemes set up at UAL since 2002 to capitalise on staff and student enterprise initiatives, develop company spin-outs and build up IP portfolios.[17]

In response to this rapid proliferation of new enterprise zones in the cultural and educational sectors, some leading progressives advocate a rearguard challenge to neoliberalisation with the aid of what MACBA's head of public programmes, Jorge Ribalta, has called his 'trustees from below' (e.g. displaced, dispossessed and previously excluded constituencies).[18] With uncanny echoes of Blairite sociologist Anthony Giddens's earlier totem 'the state without enemies', these art institutions without enemies no longer recuperate resistance or institutionalise critique but claim to operate as its facilitators – partners in its very construction. And herein lies a principle contradiction: the content of the institution's discourse can be utterly inverted in the institutional form. While formally affirming the fight against precarious labour, for example, institutions continue to maintain high levels of labour insecurity among their workers. Ctrl-i's act of refusal brought this to wider attention, but it was already the subject of earlier critiques from activist network The Chainworkers at El Precariat Social Rebel (November 2003) and Spanish Indymedia activists at EuroMayDay Barcelona (2004). All these critiques actually occurred 'within' MACBA and, to varying degrees, at the behest of the museum itself (Indymedia Barcelona for example, is said to have grown out of one of its workshops). MACBA not only 'commands' criticism but lays down the terms and conditions in which it can take place. It does it by offering its facilities and expertise, by inviting the big international celebrity activists to further politicise their 'trustees', and generally help to integrate anti-capitalist and social movements into its programme. As Gerald Raunig puts it:

> A productive game emerges here in the relationship between activists and institution, which is neither limited to a co-optation of the political by the institution, nor to a simple redistribution of resources from the progressive art institution to the political actions.[19]

This then begs the question whether, for all the autocritique conducted by institutional directors, curators and activists, for all the talk of transnational networks linking up radical reformist elements, what tangible 'progressive' change has occurred within art institutions? Or indeed, for all those on temporary, fixed term contracts, in Spanish and other European (non-art) contexts?[20] Are we just looking at institutions looking at institutions looking at institutions – churning self-reflexivity as they oversee the creation of the EU's socially conscious variant on UK/US neoliberalism.

If two earlier phases of institutional critique broadly located in the '70s and '90s have been integrated into cycles of legitimation and further disabled by the ongoing privatisation of culture and education, should we take these more recent state-funded institutionally led initiatives seriously as a 'third phase' as some have argued? Of all the interpretations put forward by eipcp 'correspondents' and associates at the 2005 conference The Future of Institutional Critique and in the first issue of the web journal *Transversal*, filmmaker Hito Steyerl's is perhaps the most plausible though by no means unproblematic.[21] She notes the integration of cultural workers into the flexible, temporary and exploitative labour conditions ushered in by neoliberalisation and claims that there is a 'need for institutions which could cater to the new needs and desires that this constituency will create'.

It's necessary here, when talking about needs, desires and constituencies, to acknowledge class struggle in these new enterprise zones/progressive art institutions and maintain clear lines of antagonism in any proposed 'third phase' of institutional critique. As ctrl-i have shown, we could start by directly confronting in-house disparities and inequities and ask why radical reformers avoid debating ongoing and often intensified labour market segmentation (i.e. the differential between permanent and temporary workers) within their own 'exemplary' cultural and educational institutions? Why do those at the top of the institutional pile and their army of new consultants continue to promote self-reflexivity and claim to facilitate dissent while acting as a buttress to elite class power? The question then is not so much whether *2015's* call for the EU 'to invest in long-term basic funding for transnational infrastructures' should be met (eipcp's continued funding suggests that it has been, in their case) but the manner and extent to which these infrastructures function in the service of capital.

Footnotes

1

Email correspondence with ctrl-i, August 2006. According to ctrl-i's account of their relations with the museum's Temporary Employment Agency, Serveis Educatius Ciut'art, SL, some of those who had spoken out against the museum were removed from their contracted positions in the 'guided tour' programme and placed in other, less publicly engaged, roles. Within two months all had left the museum. As temporary workers none had recourse to claiming 'constructive' or unfair dismissal. In UK law constructive dismissal is where an employee is moved to resign due to their employer's behaviour (and this can range from the interpersonal, harassment etc., to the structural, where the nature or description of the job changes), see http://en.wikipedia.org/wiki/Constructive_dismissal. For an online account of ctrl-i's relation to MACBA and their withdrawal letter see http://www.metamute.org/en/node/7469 and i-manifest at http://sindominio.net/ctrl-i/invert_and_subvert.html

2

The invitation to ctrl-i to participate in the Another Relationality (part 2) workshops was made by MACBA and Marcello Espósito on behalf of the now disbanded 'Faculty for Radical Aesthetics', an offshoot of the European Institute for Progressive Cultural Policies (eipcp). See the call for applications, https://lists.resist.ca/pipermail/aut-op-sy/2005-June/004311.html

3

This article is based on a text originally commissioned by *Art Monthly*, where debate on institutionalisation and so-called 'New Institutionalism' has been developed through Dave Beech's 'Institutionalisation For All', No. 294, March 2006; Peter Suchin's 'On Institutionalisation', No. 295, April 2006; Lisa Le Feuvre's 'The Institution Within', No. 297, June 2006 and Jakob Jakobsen's 'Self-Institutionalisation', No. 298, July-August 2006, as well as the conference Worlds Within Worlds: the Institutions of Art, July 2006: http://www.artmonthly.co.uk/institutions.htm

4

David Harvey. *A Brief History of Neoliberalism*, Oxford University Press, 2005, pp. 87.

5

European Cultural Policies 2015: A Report with Scenarios on the Future of Public Funding for Contemporary Art in Europe was commissioned as part of Frieze Projects and distributed free of charge at the Frieze Art Fair in October 2005. The report is also available as a pdf-file at: http://www.iaspis.com and http://www.eipcp.net

6

Maria Lind, introduction to *European Cultural Policies 2015:* The previous year Iaspis had an artists-commission project proposal rejected by Frieze Foundation. The Foundation is supported by Arts Council England and the Culture 2000 programme. The 2005 Frieze Projects were commissioned in association with Cartier and supported by Arts & Business and Calouste Gulbenkian Foundation.

7

Gerald Raunig, '2015 [Introduction]', http://eipcp.net/policies/2015/raunig/en. For Maria Lind's introduction, see http://eipcp.net/policies/2015/lind/en

8

Pierre Bourdieu and Loïc Wacquant have identified such consultants' role in granting a veneer of legitimacy to projects of the new state and business nobility. Their prototypical example was Anthony Giddens, British sociologist and ideological architect of the Third Way. See Pierre Bourdieu and Loïc Wacquant, 'Neoliberal Newspeak: Notes on the New Planetary Vulgate', *Radical Philosophy*, 108, January 2001, http://www.radicalphilosophy.com/default.asp?channel_id=2187&editorial_id=9956

9

They are listed in the 'cooperation' section of epipcp's website and stand at around 50 organisations as of March 2007,
http://eipcp.net/institute/cooperation/cooperation

10

'European Added Value' is outlined in the 'Award Criteria' section of the European Commission, Culture 2000 Specifications document,
http://ec.europa.eu/culture/eac/how_particip2000/pract_info/appel_2006_en.html

11

See Discordia exchange on progressive institutions: 'more than one shining institution',
http://www.discordia.us/scoop/story/2004/2/10/191433/396.html and Jorge Ribalta, 'Mediation and Construction of Publics. The MACBA Experience', April 2004,
http://www.republicart.net/disc/institution/ribalta01_en.htm

12

Republicart manifesto, September 2002,
http://www.republicart.net/manifesto/manifesto_en.htm and eipcp 2002 intro,
http://eipcp.net/institute/reflectionzone/eipcp2001/en

13

See Discordia,
http://www.discordia.us/scoop/story/2004/2/10/191433/396.htm

14

See MACBA Foundation
http://www.macba.es/controller.php?p_action=show_page&pagina_id=24&inst_id=15175 and 'A Widening Probe in Spain', *Newsweek Magazine*, 22 April, 2002.

15

Ned Rossiter, 'Organised Networks: Transdisciplinarity and New Institutional Forms',
http://transform.eipcp.net/correspondence/1144943951

16

'Jon Boone, 'University Spin-Outs Turn the Heads of Venture Capitalists', *Financial Times*, September 28, 2006 and and venture capital firm Quester's commentary/report into 'Building University Spin-Outs: A VC's View on Three Key Ingredients to Success', October 2006
http://www.quester.co.uk/pdfs/Building_viable_university_spinouts.pdf

17

See http://www.arts.ac.uk/business/about.htm

18

Jorge Ribalta, 'Mediation and Construction of Publics. The MACBA Experience', April 2004,
http://www.republicart.net/disc/institution/ribalta01_en.htm

19

Gerald Raunig, 'The Double Criticism of parrhesia. Answering the Question "What is a Progressive (Art) Institution?"'
http://www.republicart.net/disc/institution/raunig04_en.htm

20

Spain accounts for 31 percent of temporary workers in Europe and has more temp workers than Italy, the UK, Belgium and Sweden combined. See Sebastian Royo, 'The European Union and Economic Reforms: The case of Spain',
http://www.realinstitutoelcano.org/documentos/243.asp

21

Debates on a third 'phase' or 'wave' of institutional critique can be found in Simon Sheikh's 'Notes on Institutional Critique', Hito Steyerl's 'Institution of Critique' and Gerald Raunig's 'Instituent Practices: Fleeing, Instituting, Transforming'. All can be found at http://transform.eipcp.net/transversal/0106/raunig/en

Anthony Davies
<ajwdavies@yahoo.co.uk> is a writer and organiser

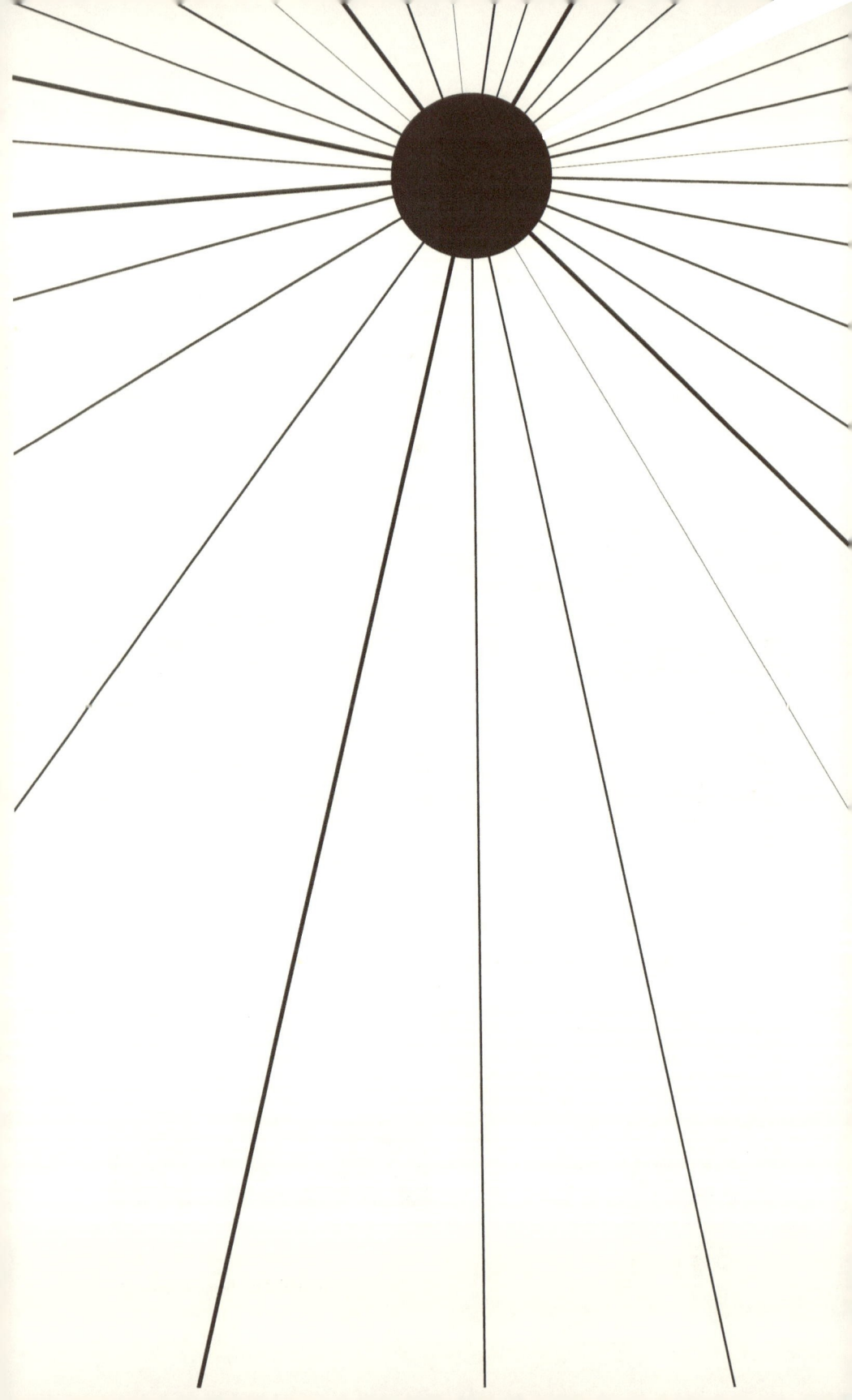

Climate for Change

13 March - 31 May 2009

Special FACT Section

FACT
FOUNDATION FOR ART AND
CREATIVE TECHNOLOGY

INTRODUCTION

Climate change isn't the only hot topic facing the planet. Environmental crisis, food crisis and housing crisis, all against the backdrop of an economic crisis that has been a long time coming.

Climate for Change is an exhibition that was conceived as a response to Liverpool's Year of the Environment. Yet at this moment in time, it is impossible to discuss the environment without contextualizing it within a wider frame of power, money and politics. Environmentalist ideologies all too often exist in a narrow framework that pits naturalism against inexorable capitalist development. But what happens when the neoliberal order begins to unravel? Who is the new enemy? Moreover, how do we enter into this debate normally reserved for the geopolitical elite?

With this backdrop, Climate for Change eschews the idea of an eco-art exhibition in favour of the establishment of a space for collective discourse and action, holistically addressing the debate about the environment. The exhibition is focused on an experiment in FACT's main gallery that uses the 'social centre' as a model, inviting groups to use FACT's space and resources to host their own events and workshops. These groups participate in what writer Simon Yuill, in an essay printed in this reader, calls distributive practices: 'a "way of doing" that seeks to propagate the knowledge and resources through which it is generated, and which itself also generates, so that others may adopt and adapt it'. Influencing as well as being influenced by networked technology:

> The principle of distributiveness entails that the practice should be self-legitimating, adoption of the practice should not be dependent on passing tests, acquiring certification or the approval of governing bodies. A distributive practice is not a doctrine or discipline, with a set of canonical principles to be adhered to, nor does it require institutional representation, such as an academic qualification, martial art, or religious practice might. It allows for unplanned future mutations and re-inventions rather than seeking to guard against them.
>
> Simon Yuill, *Survival Scrapbooks* (http://www.metamute.org, March 2006)

This exhibition posits the idea that distributive practices create networks of individuals with experience in self-organizing; providing the confidence and feeding

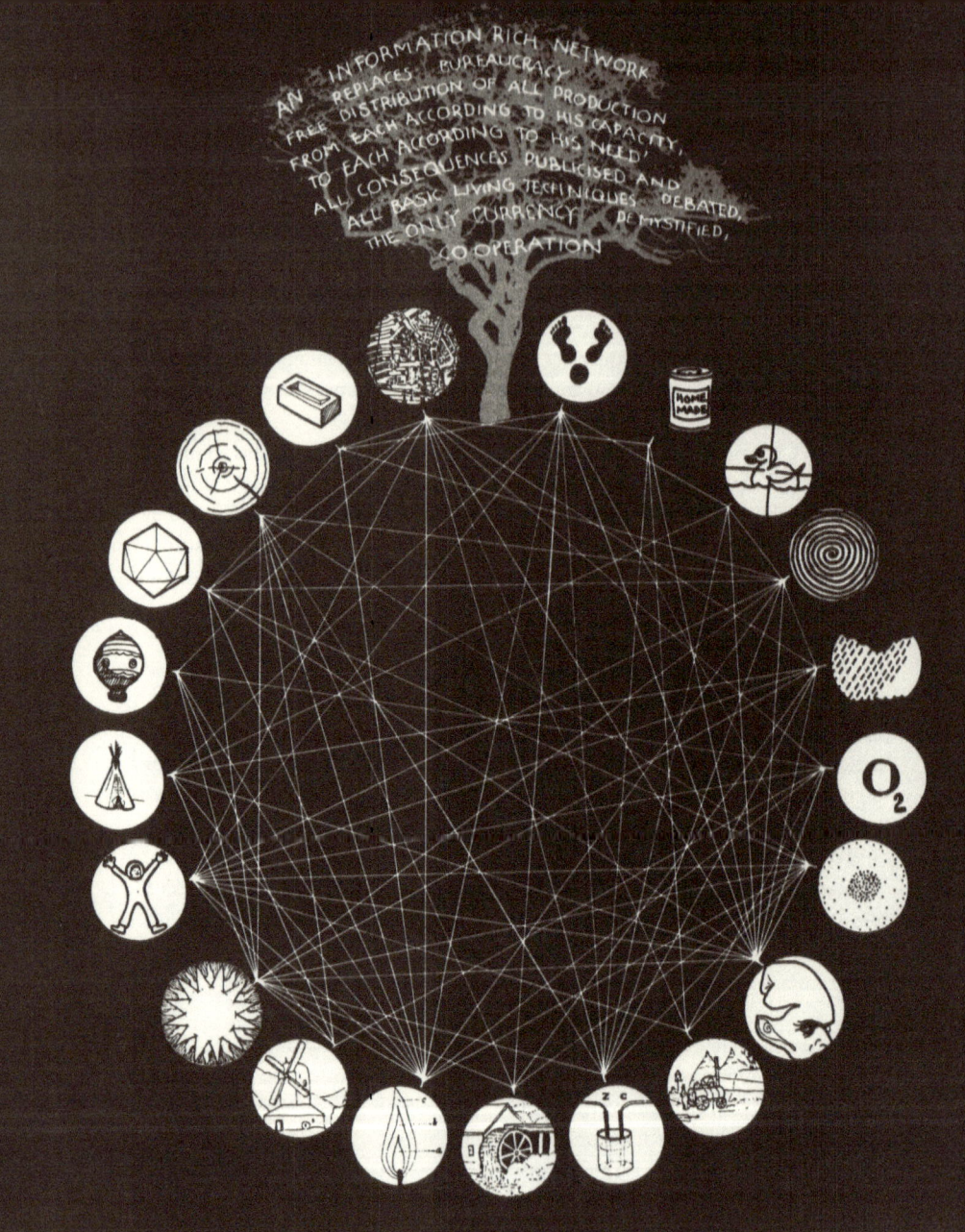

Image: Excerpt from *Survival Scrapbook #3: Energy* (1974), Stefan Szczelkun.

the imaginations that could form the foundation for real change for the environment and beyond, while contributing to current struggles and solutions.

There is a climate for change in the air. The 21st century has finally hit, having manifested itself in the peaking of trajectories that generations have taken as a given – 'peak oil' implies the hydrocarbon economy is on its last legs, while the collapse of international finance shows that 'peak credit' has also arrived. The question is: what is our collective response?

Gallery 1

A range of groups will take up residence at FACT in an environment created from the leftover building materials of 2008's Capital of Culture year. The networked activities of Merseyside are highlighted in this experiment, as FACT hands over the keys to the door and becomes a hub for meetings, socials, discussions and workshops, supporting grassroots networks to practise and imagine new models of governance and organising - live in the gallery space. Underpinning this action will be a number of artist-led activities.

New York's stages its *Sustainability Road Show* – a series of workshops and activities that are both playful and social, highlighting Eyebeam's strong media lab culture built around tinkering, hacking, making and doing. Eyebeam is North America's leading institution for producing media art and technology projects, and the road show format was conceived by their Senior Fellows as a method for taking their work out and into contact with the public. Participating artists include **Steve Lambert** who uses conversation and collective imagination in his artworks to bridge radical ideas with everyday life; **Hans-Christoph Steiner** who focuses on human perceptual capabilities, building networks with free software, and composing music with computers; and **Jeff Crouse**, who creates software and installations that highlight the absurdity of technology in culture. Through hands-on events the *Sustainability Road Show* posits that media artists working in at the intersection of art and technology, in a media arts culture steeped in a history of activism, may be well poised to contribute to sustainability's debates and solutions.

Artist **Stefan Szczelkun** presents a series of projected images from his *Survival Scrapbooks: Food, Energy and Shelter* (1972 – 1974). Originally published in the early 1970s, his three Survival Scrapbooks are DIY manuals for autonomous living, covering practical topics from 'bio-diesel-making' to 'increasing your chi'. Written just before Szczelkun joined a small eco-commune, the Scrapbooks were first published by Unicorn Bookshop in Brighton and experimented with the book format – hole punches on the pages allowed for collecting in a binder and re-editing with other material. The books, along with Szczelkun's later work with Scratch Orchestra and the mail art community, saw him as an offline pioneer of pre-internet collaborative tools and information sharing systems.

Climate for Change 13 March - 31 May 2009

Mute Magazine Contributing Editor **Anthony Iles** revisits the magazine's climate change issue – *Mute* Vol 2 #5 'It's Not Easy Being Green', from May 2007 – to update it in light of changing perspectives on finance, capital and current affairs. Iles curates a discussion series that runs on evenings and weekends throughout the exhibition that includes a walking tour of Liverpool with researcher Kim Singleton and activist Leo Singer; a workshop challenging green orthodoxies with *Shift* magazin e & No Borders Manchester; and a discussion on how financial crisis impacts cultural practice and what would be a 'sustainable' alternative. A concurrent screening series seeks to expand the term 'environment' to include other man-made ill effects.

In addition to these events, Gallery 1 will house a loose and rotating line-up of Liverpool artist residencies, to support and encourage Liverpool's creative networks. Residents include British-born Chinese artist **Kao-Oi Jay Yung**, underground creative network **The Kazamier**, Beccy Williams of the crafts group and self-run studio space **C.U.T.S.**, and artist-led environmental group **The Gaia Project**, in partnership with **L@tE**.

Media Lounge, Atrium & Public Realm

In the Media Lounge, Copenhagen-based art and architecture collective **N55** set up *SHOP* (2002 -), an exchange area with its own alternative economy, where visitors can swap, borrow or use donated items. An outline of *SHOP*, among other projects such as *WORK, LAND,* and *FACTORY*, is written up in a technical manual freely available on the N55 website for anyone to use to stage their own iteration of the project. The manual specifies that *SHOP* is made up of anything that people would like to offer the shop, which are labelled in different categories: that they can only be used at *SHOP* (yellow tag), borrowed (magenta tag), or they can be used, borrowed, swapped or if necessary, taken (cyan tag). For the Climate for Change exhibition, N55 have added another category to the things in *SHOP* – black tags are tagged on things that have precipitated, aided or provoked a change in a person's life. A thread running through much of the collective's work, *SHOP* encourages community self-reliance through collaboration and sharing outside the motivation of profit.

Nearby in FACT's Atrium, *Ghana Think Tank* (2008 -) is a globally distributed network of think tanks creating strategies to resolve local problems. Created by **Christopher Robbins, Matey Odonkor** and **John Ewing**, the project asks visitors to submit their local problems which will be given to think tanks in Ghana, Cuba, El Salvador, Serbia, Mexico and Ethiopia to solve – groups formed

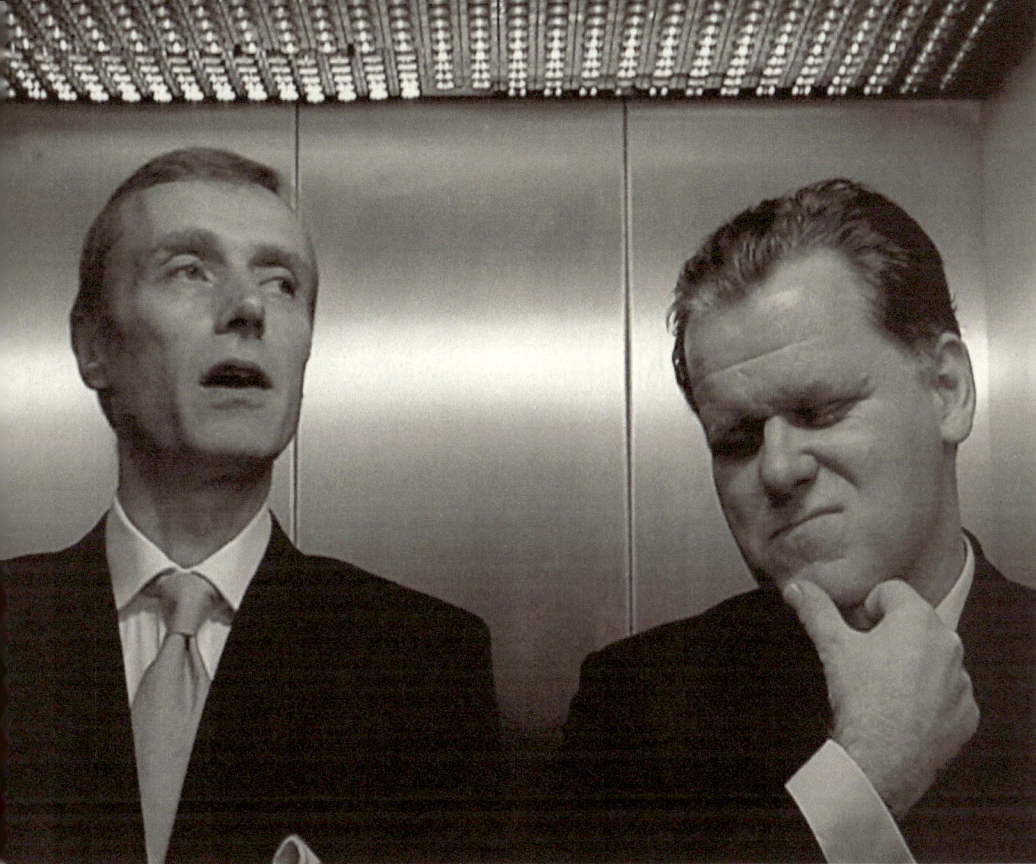

Image: Still from *Crisis in the Credit System* (2008), Melanie Gilligan

from the artists' own networks. The artists will work with local residents and the problem's owners to enact and document solutions provided. While the obvious role reversal – think tanks are typically understood to originate in richer Western countries to solve the problems of others – is an amusing thought, more than that the exercise provides surprising, if sometimes simple, insights from the challenge of a different cultural perspective.

Gallery 2

Alongside these active experiments are a series of works that situate the viewer simultaneously in the future and the present, underlining the current climate as one of change – a place for reflection on future as self-fulfilling prophecy.

Melanie Gilligan's film *Crisis in the Credit System* (2008), originally commissioned and produced by Artangel Interaction, is a fictional four-part drama that tells a

Climate for Change 13 March - 31 May 2009

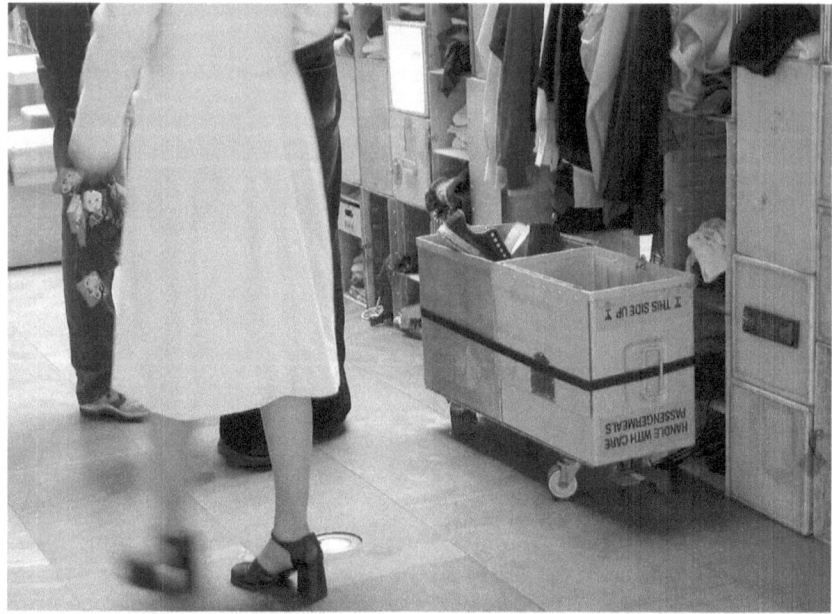

Image: N55, *SHOP*, (2002- ongoing)

story of five investment bank employees asked to brainstorm solutions to today's dangerous financial climate at a company retreat. The role-play exercise starts out with typical 'double or nothing' approaches – manipulating share prices, developing complex financial instruments – before becoming increasingly bizarre, leading ultimately to disturbing conclusions. While firmly rooted in the present, the film paints the picture of an imaginary future that unsettles even its own City worker protagonists.

Copies of a spoofed *New York Times – Special Edition* (2008) newspaper declaring the Iraq war over will get a further outing at FACT. Six months in the making, 1.2 million copies of the paper were handed out in major cities across the US on in November 2008. Created to challenge the political discussion around the Iraq war and prompt a newly-elected Barack Obama to keep his campaign promises, the paper attempts to realize a self-fulfilling prophecy by elaborating on a fictional, but possible, future. Articles spell out a liberal utopia of national health care, the abolition of corporate lobbying, a maximum wage for C.E.O.s, and, the article's centerpiece, the end of the Iraq war. The action, credited to 'thousands of volunteers', sparked widespread news coverage.

Berlin-based duo **Nik Kosmas** and **Daniel Keller (AIDS 3D)** will unveil *Forever* (2009), a new installation alluding to a post-apocalyptic future where

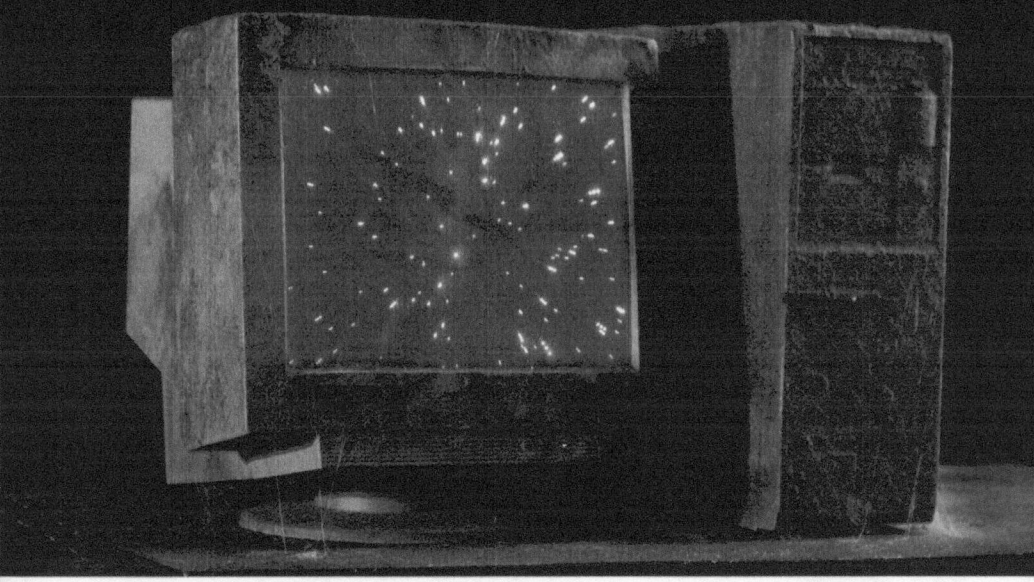

Image: Daniel Keller and Nik Kosmos, *Forever*, (2009)

machines remain as beautiful relics of our former glory. While the work is dystopian – set in an empty future where all that remains is a burned-out computer terminal running a pathetic, looping version of the classic Windows 98 stars screensaver – its underlying messages are ones of techno-utopianism. The work is fed on the optimistic concepts of science fiction diehards: technological singularity, a theoretical future point of unprecedented progress, where machines that are even slightly more intelligent than humans can lead us down unknowable paths; omega point, the idea that the universe is developing towards more complexity and consciousness, drawn by a supreme point that is transcendent; and the hedonistic imperative, a bio-engineered utopia where all pain and suffering is abolished. Yet while the work articulates the point at which these hopeful concepts are abandoned in environmental crisis, war, and the breakdown of global economies, it also conspicuously uses outdated technology as its centerpiece - an instantly recognizable retro screensaver burned into popular consciousness (the duo use technology symbols like others use religious or pagan ones). In this way the work draws the point of failure in our past, giving us the subtle hope these sci-fi aspirations may be realized after all.

Together, these three works offer visions of the future, their multiplicity of views conveying a subtle sense of urgency that underlines the main exhibition, prompting radical action now towards defining the correct paths.

Heather Corcoran, Curator

Subscription offer

10% off the Mute catalogue

Subscribe to Mute and guarantee to be the first in line for our quarterly collection of provocative articles on culture, politics and technology. What's even better, subscribe now and not only get Mute delivered straight to your door but receive 10% off of our new Catalogue, including magazine back issues and titles from the OpenMute print on demand press. That's a year or more of discounts on books, back issues and Mute special projects. Below is just a small selection from the broad range of products on offer.

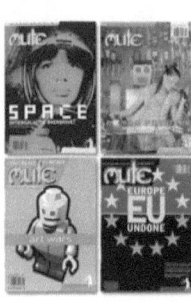

Find yourself a Mute short of a full set? Take advantage of our subscriber offer to get 10% off. If you missed out on earlier formats, Mute Back Issues collections offer sets of back issues for only **£35**/collection (which means **£31.50** if you subscribe). Mute's new collections – grouped according to the magazine's successive formats – make it easy to build or complete your very own Mute library*.

- Back Issues I: the Broadsheet (pilot-issue 7, safely packed in two unique pink folders, 'back pack 1 & 2')
- Back Issues II: the Glossies (issues 8-24)
- Back Issues III: Coffee Table (issues 25-29)
- Back Issues IV: the POD (current volume, issues 0-7).

*We regret to say that none of these include issue 9, which is now sold out.

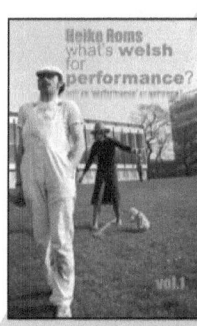

Heike Roms' *What's Welsh for Performance? Beth yw 'performance' yn Gymraeg?* **An Oral History of Performance Art in Wales 1968-2008**
For more than forty years artists have been creating performances, happenings and other time-based art in Wales, yet their work remains largely confined to half-remembered anecdotes, rumours and hearsay. *What's Welsh for Performance?* tries to uncover Wales's hidden history of performance in conversations with key artists who have shaped this history since 1968.
Price £10 £9

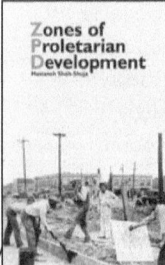

Shah-Shuja Mastaneh's *Zones of Proletarian Development*
Zones of Proletarian Development is an attempt to theorise the anti-capitalist movement from a neo-Vygotskian perspective. It analyses a series of proletarian activities including recent May Day celebrations in London, carnivalesque football riots in Iran, the anti-poll-tax rebellion and the anti-war movement. Concluding by looking at past and current proletarian organisations, this book makes a number of proposals for future modes of organising conducive to radical consciousness and autonomous activity.
Price £15 £13.50

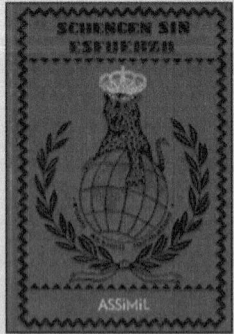

Vahida Ramujkic's *Schengen with Ease*
'Extra-comunitarios', or citizens of non-European countries, have the 'extra' bureaucratic task of changing their status to one that will allow them to move and work 'freely' within the European Union. All the required steps are taught through lessons like those found in foreign language skill books, comparing the administrative language of European immigration legislation to an unknown language that has to be mastered first in order to assimilate in to a new environment, receiving determined status.
Price £8.29 £7.46

Download the complete catalogue at metamute.org/catalogue
Or contact lois@metamute.org +44 (0)20 7377 6949 for a printed copy

MUTE

Subscription Rates:

	individual		institutional/company	
	4 issues (1 year)	8 issues (2 years)	4 issues (1 year)	8 issues (2 years)
uk	☐ £20	☐ £38	☐ £35	☐ £67
europe	☐ €28	☐ €52	☐ €48	☐ €91
usa/mx	☐ $40	☐ $75	☐ $70	☐ $133
row	☐ €34	☐ €60	☐ €54	☐ €102

Please tick the appropriate box.

I wish to pay by cheque/credit card.
☐ I enclose a cheque (GBP) made payable to Mute.
☐ Please charge my

☐ Visa ☐ Access ☐ Mastercard ☐ Switch

Card no. ☐☐☐☐ ☐☐☐☐ ☐☐☐☐ ☐☐☐☐
Expiry date ☐☐ / ☐☐
[Switch only] Issue number ☐☐   Start date ☐☐ / ☐☐
Security code ☐☐☐

Signature _____

name _____
address _____
_____
_____
town/city _____
post code _____
country _____
tel _____
email _____

Or call our credit card hotline
Tel +44 (0)20 7377 6949
Fax +44 (0)20 7377 9520

Online metamute.org/shop
Email mute@metamute.org
Skype mute.london

POST TO: MUTE,
Unit 9, The
Whitechapel Centre,
85 Myrdle St.,
London E1 1HQ, UK

www.ingramcontent.com/pod-product-compliance
Lightning Source LLC
Chambersburg PA
CBHW031921240526
45464CB00021B/625